HOW I MET
MY SON

HOW I MET MY SON

A JOURNEY THROUGH ADOPTION

ROSALIND POWELL

BLINK
bringing you closer

Published by Blink Publishing
3.25, The Plaza,
535 Kings Road,
Chelsea Harbour,
London, SW10 0SZ

www.blinkpublishing.co.uk

facebook.com/blinkpublishing
twitter.com/blinkpublishing

978-1-910536-55-1

A CIP catalogue of this book is available from the British Library.

Typeset by www.envydesign.co.uk

Printed and bound by Clays Ltd, St Ives Plc

3 5 7 9 10 8 6 4 2

Papers used by Blink Publishing are natural, recyclable products made from
wood grown in sustainable forests. The manufacturing processes conform to the
environmental regulations of the country of origin.

Blink Publishing is an imprint of the Bonnier Publishing Group
www.bonnierpublishing.co.uk

To my darling boy and his lovely dad

Foreword

by Satwinder Sandhu, Director of Operations at
The Homefinding & Fostering Agency, and Former
Director of Adoption and Fostering at PACT

I had just come back to work in London, after a year in Australia, when I started working with Ros and Harry. Like me, they loved to travel and enjoyed talking about a whole manner of interesting subjects, so our time together was always well spent. In our case, though, I was their social worker from the adoption agency, so the type of journey I joined them on was quite different to visiting far-flung continents. This one was all about finding them a child to come and live with them – in their own home.

I never imagined we would be at this stage of that same journey so many years later, when I would be reading about the whole experience of adoption from Ros' own perspective, but here we are.

For me as a social worker specialising in adoption and fostering, I am in a unique and privileged position. I get to know people in a way that perhaps even those closest to them don't, and I get to be a part of their family as it is created or expanded. It is an absolutely fascinating role when you break it down to those bare bones. I do not know why I was drawn to such work, but I have always loved it. As a social worker and as a manager it has certainly provided me with a way to connect to, and be part of, future generations without having a child of my own.

I firmly believe that adoption gives children in need a lifeline. It is not about 'saving' them like a Hollywood film might have us believe, but giving them an opportunity to be part of a family and to be their own person. Blood, water, nature and nurture may be important discussion points to some folk but to me adoption is all about chemistry. The best relationships in life start with this in abundance and adopting a child is no different.

Sadly, in 2015 adoption seems to be on the decline in Britain. That may change but for now greater emphasis on children remaining in extended family arrangements means that numbers of children needing to be adopted have dropped further. However, for me, adoption is, and always will be a valid and positive option for children.

I always think of the film *Sliding Doors* when I hear people being cynical about adoption and calling it outdated. What other route might the lives of the hundreds of children I've worked with over the years have taken had they not been adopted? Would they be better or worse off? I conclude better off. Why? I now work for a The Homefinding & Fostering Agency. We specialise in permanence through foster care, and do this very well, but what I also see (more than I would like to) is young people and foster carers walking away from their relationship, after years together.

This usually happens when emotions run high and things become 'challenging'. Whilst some adoptions also 'break down', I cannot help but think that our young people would have been more secure had they, too, been adopted and not deemed 'too old' or 'too complex'.

The legality of adoption is like the legality of marriage. It binds people together, meaning they usually think twice if they want to separate from that relationship. Therefore, to me, adoption is not a 'better' option but it is certainly more secure and truly creates a lifelong relationship.

Anyway, back to Ros and Harry. I was just in my mid-twenties when I worked with them. I was finding my stride as a social worker, and they certainly put me through my paces, especially Ros. I really liked them both and this made the job a whole lot easier, as in the role I really had to be their strongest advocate and champion. This was before the days of social media and online profiles of children needing adoption. It was hard work to find a child that adopters-in-waiting would not only be interested in but then also selected for. I had no concerns about their suitability but finding the right child for them was another important part of the journey, one that came with many bumps, wrong turns and roads to nowhere.

Ros talks about these experiences in this memoir with almost as much emotion as she and Harry expressed at the time, but of course we all know there is a son at the end of this journey because she tells us in the title. When I heard about Gabriel, though, I instantly knew he could be their child.

Ros' account of their journey through infertility and the long road to adoption is honest, insightful, funny and at times painful, but ultimately it's a celebration of Gabriel, a very special boy who will one day be a young man and possibly a parent himself. I know Ros thought long and hard about putting his life into words, but I encouraged her to do so as I believed it would be valuable for not only him, but many others embarking on a similar path to her's and Harry's.

This memoir deals with a range of issues that affect adopters as well as the realities of living in modern-day multi-cultural Britain, and it does so honestly, making the book a great read. It's a must read for everyone, but particularly anyone who is thinking about adopting or has adopted, or who is simply, like us social workers, plain old nosey and want to read about the experience.

It's a wonderful journey to have been part of and it was certainly touching to relive it. I hope you enjoy it too and feel the love that Ros and Harry have for Gabriel, their son.

Satwinder Sandhu
December, 2015

Preface

I felt sorry for the GP. She was only a locum so it can't have been easy for her telling us, happily ignorant, that we could never conceive naturally. Too stunned to ask questions, we said nothing. We didn't even reach out to hold hands. She gently talked us through the results of our fertility tests and explained that our only hope of getting pregnant was through IVF. But I wasn't really listening: my world had just fallen apart.

I started to cry as soon as we left the surgery and walked up the hill to the car. It was the first week of January 1998 and the sky was granite grey. Harry and I sat in silence for a minute. He looked at me and said, because there was nothing else to say, 'What's the matter?' before promptly bursting into tears.

The next day Harry's sister Debbie came round with her baby daughter to visit. I left him in the living room to break the news and I went to bed. Her happiness fed my misery. I thought I'd never stop crying. Grief came in tall waves, bringing with it a profound sense of loss, as well as fury at not being able to do the simplest, most natural thing for a woman.

I had a womb that would never be used.

Chapter One

Eleven years later I'm sitting at the table in our breakfast room, nagging my son Gabriel to finish his tea. He's spent the last 30 minutes pushing a half-eaten fishcake around his plate while fashioning an exploding weapon from a paperclip. From nowhere, he says, 'Do you wish you'd never got me?'

'What do you mean?' I ask, stunned but curious to find out where this is going.

'Do you wish you'd got someone else?'

'No,' I say, trying to sound nonchalant, my heart pounding, 'why, do *you* wish I had?'

'No,' he says good-naturedly, and zaps me with his paperclip.

I still can't work out what the conversation was *really* about, or on how deep a level Gabriel was asking me these questions. He'd made it sound such a casual, throwaway remark that I was almost fooled. But then again he was

1

only six and a half and although he knew he was adopted, I'm not sure how much of it he understood.

Do I wish I'd 'got' someone else? 'No' isn't a big enough answer. Gabriel feels so completely my – our – child that I can't imagine anyone else in his place. He looks nothing like me, or Harry – his skin is a beautiful light brown, ours a mottled pink. He's a light-hearted optimist with a good ear for music, neither attributes we share. But sometimes when I look at him I see Harry: the way he points with his middle finger, or can fix a leaky tap. And we can make each other laugh like drains. No one can infuriate or frustrate me more. But then, I don't love anyone else in the way I love him.

All those years ago, in another lifetime, I thought my chances of becoming a mother had been taken away. I wanted a family but didn't know how to find one. This is the story of my eight-year-long quest to find that family and how we eventually came to adopt our son.

It's no fairytale, rescuing orphans from poverty. Nor is this a misery memoir of a life ruined by a dysfunctional child. It's not triumph over tragedy, or romantic, glamorous or gruesome – well, maybe only in parts. In many ways it's a universal story of parenthood – the end result is the same, it's just that our journey was different. There are so many books written about pregnancy, childbirth and babies, but not so many about adoption, or that are positive. When we embarked on the process I was desperate to hear and read about other people's experiences, but found it difficult to relate to most of the books out there. I wanted to read an honest, warts-and-all account that didn't put me off, so I decided to write one myself.

* * *

I'd always assumed I'd have children, but never gave it much thought. I didn't hunger for them, or plan my life around them. As a girl I played mums and babies with my friends and imagined one day I'd have a family like the one I grew up in: mum, dad, two children, one dog. But as a teenager the fear of an unplanned pregnancy loomed like a spectre. This fear continued throughout my twenties until, growing into my thirties, I knew that if I ever got pregnant by accident, I would keep the baby for fear that it might be my last chance to have a family.

Not that I particularly wanted one, and nor did any of my friends. We were the generation destined to lead a different life to our mothers, to bypass the drudgery of housewifery and motherhood. University educated, we had our hearts set on careers in the arts or media – not for us the fusty worlds of law, commerce or medicine. But we weren't completely driven by our careers either. Money wasn't a motivation, but being hip and slightly bohemian was.

I was thirty when I met Harry and had just changed careers from arts administration to journalism. I'd never lived with a boyfriend before, so it came as a shock when he moved in after a month. I knew this was 'It' but was terrified I'd mess it up, or that he'd soon discover his mistake. After three years, he still hadn't and so we decided, with some trepidation, to start 'trying' to get pregnant. Even then I feared it wasn't going to work. About ten years before I'd had my birth chart read by a skinny hippy in Bristol who told me I might have difficulty having children. I had, she said, a 'creative block', adding that one of the most creative things we can do in life is

3

make a child. At the time it felt as if she'd cast a dark spell like some wicked fairy and the sense of foreboding never quite left me. After ten successive months, Harry and I had still created nothing.

Every month I'd wait with anticipation for my period not to arrive and every month it did. Disappointment would descend with a dull thud. The times in between I'd be sensitive to every possible symptom – tender bosoms, a bloated stomach, feeling tired. I peed on sticks that told me when I was ovulating and we obediently had sex during our window of fertilisation opportunity: missing a go could mean missing a baby. One month I was two days' late. We were on holiday in Scotland, visiting lochs, climbing hills and drinking coffee in cafés in Glasgow, and dared to get a little excited, considering the possibilities. I felt scared – was this it? Was I ready? I was almost relieved when my period started.

I'm not sure how much I'd thought through my reasons for wanting a child; it felt instinctive. It wasn't until several years later when we were going through the adoption process that we really had to analyse our motives for wanting a family. Nor had I really considered the practicalities, the effect it would have on my life. If anything, I remember feeling slightly threatened by the possibility of a new person being introduced into our lives. I'd have to share my relationship. Of course I would have coped; you have no choice. Even now I sometimes feel relieved that we didn't have to go through the slightly mad, sleep-deprived newborn baby phase when the only mission in life is to keep your child alive, although I often tell Gabriel how I wish I'd known him as a newborn.

But back then we just wanted to reach the first hurdle. The GP sent us off for tests. I tried not to take them too seriously; I'd laugh at Harry having to give his sperm specimens in small jars, and reassured myself that plenty of couples took time to conceive and that ten months wasn't long in the great scheme of things. But I sort of knew somewhere, something was wrong.

Being told I couldn't have children naturally felt like I'd been sentenced to a lifetime of grief. I can't say I miss having my own, biological child now because I don't. But what I do miss is the experience of pregnancy and childbirth, the fact that I will never know how it feels to grow and carry a baby, to feel its skin against mine, stroke downy hair and breathe that milky smell. Or place my hands on a gloriously round stomach and feel for bumps, kicks and hiccups. Sometimes I can be reminded of that loss when I least expect it. I was once with a group of friends who were swapping lurid tales of giving birth. I was listening in the detached sort of way that you do when you can't share or contribute to a conversation until one of them turned to me and said, laughing, 'Don't worry, you haven't missed anything.' I can recover quickly from that sort of thoughtless insensitivity – it was such a clanger it was almost funny, and I didn't even bother responding. But she was wrong: I've missed so much.

After our heartbreaking test results I sprang into organisational mode, booking an appointment with a consultant at the Assisted Conception Unit at our local hospital in February 1998 and reading from cover to cover *The Infertility Companion*, a practical guide written by someone who'd successfully conceived through IVF.

It became my bible. I discovered that there is a one-in-five chance of successfully conceiving a baby through IVF. For older women – and at 34, I was definitely considered 'older' – the chance was considerably slimmer.

The clinic's waiting room, a grim corridor, was lined with pictures of smiling babies: their success stories. A queue of men and women at varying stages of hope, disappointment and infertility sat and talked to their partners in hushed tones, though not to the other waiting strangers, bonded as they were by an experience too painful and intimate to share. Our consultant was an attractive woman in her late fifties with a kind, intelligent face, who was reassuringly calm and warm. She explained that we'd have to wait two-and-a-half years to receive free treatment on the NHS – time we didn't have – so we booked to be 'self-financing' instead, which meant we could start that summer. Luckily our GP's surgery agreed to pay for the drugs (the most expensive part of the procedure) and we stumped up the £1,250 treatment fee. That day our consultant gave us what was probably the most useful piece of advice throughout our entire two years of treatment: 'It really helps if your whole identity isn't tied up with fertility,' she told us. 'Try and feel positive about yourself and other aspects of your life.'

Having taken the first step, we decided to celebrate. In April of that year we flew to Tucson, Arizona, and were married in the Sonoran Desert in the shade of a giant cactus. Our witnesses were two American friends, Shannon and David, who drove us in a battered old camper van to the spot we'd reccied the day before. A bearded hippy Reverend carried out the service, bringing along a posy of wild flowers that perfectly matched my gold silk dress and kitten heels. We drank champagne in the desert sun and danced to Elvis Presley playing on an ancient tape recorder before driving down to the old copper town of Bisbee on the Mexican border for our honeymoon night. We were starring in our own road movie and life felt good.

After a three-week honeymoon in California we came back home to London with a bump. Life was busy – I was freelancing, dividing my time between a weekly magazine, whose editor knew what I was going through, and a monthly women's glossy, whose editor had no idea. I'd flit from interviewing actresses, comedians, soap stars and footballers to lesbian mothers, betrayed lovers and anorexic daughters, all the while keeping a professional lid on the drama that was playing out in my own life.

At home I probably wasn't the easiest person to be around. As much as our wedding celebration had lifted my spirits and strengthened our commitment to each other, the pain of infertility was ever-present and could throw me into a pit of sadness, self-pity and seething rage. I'd look at pregnant women and think, 'How did they do that?' It infuriated me when people assumed that treatment would automatically lead to success. Even one of our GPs blithely informed us with a wave of her hand, 'Oh, everyone gets pregnant with IVF.' If friends didn't respond or gauge my feelings correctly, I'd lash out, especially at those closest to me. Shortly after our test results my dearest and oldest friend didn't phone me for two days. When she did, she admitted she hadn't known what to say. 'You're my best friend but you're not very good at it,' I snapped, making her cry.

One night I exploded in fury when Harry told me he'd

invited a friend – then six months' pregnant – to stay with us the night of the celebratory post-wedding reception we were organising. We'd also be playing host in our small flat to another visibly pregnant friend and her year-old son. 'What are we?' I shouted, 'a bloody Mother and Baby group?' I knew I couldn't avoid children and babies, or our friends who were beginning to start families of their own for the rest of my life but I wanted to be able to do so in my own time, when I felt strong and tolerant enough. But Harry felt differently. He told me that he wanted to block those feelings out; he wanted to be around other people's kids because he didn't want to feel bitter. His approach was clearly more mature and forgiving than mine. I'm not proud of the way I sometimes felt, which now seems so defensive, but that was how I was: it was part of my experience, part of the process.

* * *

That July I started our first round of IVF treatment feeling not so much positive as furtive. We'd been talked through all the hormonal drug treatment I'd be taking: the first was a nasal spray which prevented ovulation and simulated menopause; the second was a course of injections which stimulated follicle development in the ovaries (leading to more eggs being produced than in a normal cycle); then a final, one-off injection which caused the eggs to ripen, ready for collection and insemination by the sperm, at which stage Harry would have to give a sample. His contribution up until that point would be minimal. The whole process could take anything from six to eight weeks. We were also talked through the options for any spare embryos we might produce, and asked whether we wanted any surplus to be put in the deep freezer for future use. 'Embryo Cryopreservation' was the medical term. Dazzled by science, we agreed.

Meanwhile I was struggling with an innate inertia. For a year now we'd been trying to get pregnant, for test results, for treatment to start; life had been put on hold and my enthusiasm drained. It was hard to feel motivated. Overshadowing everything was the spectre of uncertainty and constant undertow of tension. It got worse when I started taking the drugs. I knew they'd have possible side effects – including mood swings, fatigue and depression – as well as menopausal symptoms such as hot flushes and insomnia. But I'd been experiencing most of them without the help of artificial stimulus. Every morning I woke up feeling like Robert De Niro in *Taxi Driver* – 'You talkin' to me?'

I developed trolley rage. It was a particularly busy Saturday in Sainsbury's when I accused a woman of stealing the trolley I'd been filling with my week's groceries. We stood in the wine and spirits aisle, battling it out as embarrassed shoppers sidled past. 'Oh God, I've got a right nutter here,' I thought, speaking to her loudly and slowly so she'd understand. Suddenly she produced a carrier bag and began packing up my food. 'Right,' I announced, flouncing off, 'I'm getting the manager.' En route I discovered my own, half-filled abandoned trolley several aisles back by the eggs. Mortified, I hunted down my victim to apologise. 'Thank you,' she smiled, more graciously than I would have done. 'I thought I was having another senior moment.'

Work was frantic – the glossy monthly had asked if I'd be interested in a full-time job so I was trying hard to make a good impression when all I wanted to do was lie on the sofa all day. We were also attempting to re-home our mad sheepdog Bob, with whom we'd been struggling for four years. One weekend we'd taken him to meet a potential new family in the Norfolk countryside, where – in just one day – he surpassed himself in atrocities, frightening the cows, upsetting their dog (so badly that it sought refuge on a lily pad in their garden pond), biting their son's hand and trying to make a run for it after pooing on their kitchen floor. Nothing was running smoothly; everything, it seemed, was sent to try us.

Meanwhile my body wasn't responding well to the drugs. A scan had shown that I'd also developed a cyst the size of a small plum on one of my ovaries. When I next rang the hospital to make an appointment I complained about feeling fed up. 'Don't worry,' said the woman at the other end of the line. 'Husbands often phone in to say their wives are refusing treatment and threatening to come off the course.' I chatted to her for a while, thanking her at the end for being so helpful.

'What's your name?' I asked.

'Emma,' she replied.

'What do you do?'

'I'm the receptionist.'

'There you go,' I thought, 'I'm shameless, I seek solace everywhere.'

That week we went to visit my friend Jo and her ten-month-old baby. It left us both feeling raw. Ella was a gorgeous child and Jo was very happy – we wanted one just like her. It was painful watching Harry put on her little socks and shoes. I knew he'd make a great father, and I couldn't bear the thought of him being denied the chance.

Finally, about two weeks overdue, my body responded to the first course of drugs and I was ready to go onto the next: daily injections into my thigh. There was no way I could inject myself, so that task fell to Harry, who practised his technique on an orange. At the next appointment our consultant and the embryologist argued over whether we should switch treatments and have the more complicated (and expensive) ICSI (intracytoplasmic sperm injection) in which a sperm is injected directly into the egg to ensure fertilisation, so increasing the chances of pregnancy. They both turned to me and asked what I thought. I said I'd gone past the point of caring and that having a baby at the end of it all felt like a sideline. That brought the discussion to an abrupt close. I then went off to have my cyst seen to, for which I was trussed up like an old carcass and pierced with a long needle. I went into work afterwards feeling like a walking pin cushion.

During this time I should probably have given up alcohol but that felt like a sacrifice too far. I got drunk just once, at a friend's wedding in Suffolk. It wasn't pretty. Mid-reception, we had to slope out for my injection, sitting like two junkies in the car park as I hoisted up my posh frock and Harry tried to keep his hand steady with the needle he'd prepared earlier. It felt seedy and ridiculous. *Snorting, Jacking Up and Jerking Off* struck me as a good title for a book, should I ever write one.

At the beginning of September, the day arrived for my

egg collection – or 'harvest', as it was quaintly called. A previous scan had shown that I had what looked like 15 eggs to collect, which was a positive result. That night I took my final injection – I was glad to see the back of those needles – and went to bed early. I felt scared: about the future, the weight of disappointment if it didn't go well, and about the operation, however minor. On arrival, Harry had to give another sperm sample in a grim little room with a chair and a few dirty, tatty magazines. Then we went into the theatre, where I was given a painkiller, and a local anaesthetic, which made me feel as if I was floating on a bed of cotton wool. It was uncomfortable rather than painful as one by one each egg was removed. When I got up to walk my legs felt like jelly. I spent the rest of the day on the sofa with a hot water bottle, watching TV. Meanwhile, in a little Petri dish on the seventh floor of the hospital, my eggs were being introduced to Harry's sperm to see if any of them fertilised. If they did, the resulting embryo would be implanted in my womb.

The following morning the embryologist phoned. His first words were, 'It's not good news.' Only one of the eggs had fertilised, but it was looking abnormal. The test now was whether it divided into two or four cells by the next day, meaning it was developing as it should.

'Maybe it's a fighter,' I joked, but he didn't respond.

'This is bloody awful,' I added.

'Yes, well imagine what it's like to have to phone people up,' he said.

I sympathised – more fool me. I got off the phone and looked up in the dictionary what our fertilised egg was called – a 'zygote'. When it divides, it's called cleaving.

'*Cleaving Zygotes* would be a good name for a book,' I thought, 'should I ever write one.'

That night we went out for dinner with my mum and sister, which saved us from sitting at home, staring at each other. On the way home we passed the hospital and sent encouraging thoughts to our genetic cluster sitting in its Petri dish.

Our consultant phoned at 9am to tell us our embryo hadn't made it. Harry was a bit tearful but I felt strangely numb, as if I'd fallen into a strange 'don't care, won't care' state. I wished we'd got further down the road, if only to give my body the chance to welcome our baby-in-progress. If my womb had experienced it once, I reasoned, it would be better prepared for the next time and not expel it from the shock of the unknown and unfamiliar. There was no logic to my thoughts, just a naive, almost mystical interpretation of how my body might work.

* * *

I didn't get the job at the women's glossy – the editor left and the position was frozen. Then Bob died. We'd finally entrusted him to a dogs' home to be re-housed and apparently he'd become increasingly aggressive and had had to be put down. Feeling personally responsible, Harry was inconsolable. We decided to leave further fertility treatment for five months, booking in for ICSI the following year. My body had taken a pounding and I wanted to give it a rest; now wasn't the right time.

The following March we started the second round of treatment. This time it was different, both physically and emotionally. My body responded better to the drugs and

I had less of a temper, but more inertia. I felt in a state of 'existence' – not happy, not sad, not moving forward. Just static. Life was on hold once more.

A few days later Harry and I were pacing the flat like a couple of bored apes, waiting for the call to tell us whether any of the eggs had fertilised. This time around we were lucky: we had seven embryos. I felt relieved that we'd come further than last time, that we'd proved we could create something together, however fragile. I kept wishing there was something I could do to prepare my body, to make their home more comfortable so that at least one of them would want to stay.

The next day we went into hospital for the embryo transfer, where three of the best-quality embryos were put back in my womb. It was impossible not to see them as our babies. We were shown them on a screen and they looked like tiny cauliflower florets, or dividing bubbles. Rather flippantly, I named them Flopsy, Mopsy and Topsy and then worried in case they'd heard and taken offence. To ease their transition we played Tony Bennett on a tape recorder. We were even offered a video of them – a new service provided by the hospital. I joked that we could give it to our performance artist friend to use in one of his shows – I could be the ultimate showbiz mum and put my embryos on the stage. It was a cheap joke but it made us laugh.

I had to fight the urge to lie in a darkened room for two weeks when my period either would, or wouldn't start. My yoga teacher had told me to visualise the embryos in a safe place, so I imagined a harbour with tiny boats and fishermen's cottages. But life, and work, went on.

One afternoon I was sent off to Hertfordshire to interview an international footballer and his girlfriend. In four hours neither the photographer, the make-up artist nor myself were offered so much as a glass of water. At one point they disappeared to the bathroom for 20 minutes. In the end I had to knock on the door to get them out.

'What the hell am I doing here?' I thought, quietly despairing.

The nurse had told me it would take around five days for the embryos to implant and up until then I'd felt reasonably calm, even positive. But Day Five arrived and I began to feel very un-pregnant. I'd woken up feeling awful, having dreamt that Harry had disappeared. I kicked him in my sleep. I wanted a sign – for my bosoms to feel sore, or to feel queasy... even just tired. Nothing. My mood turned desperate. Mum left work and came round. She told me she kept dreaming she was pregnant. My sister rang, offering to pay for Harry and me to go on holiday. That night I went to bed and urged my embryos to stay: they'd be so loved, I told them.

But they didn't listen. On Day Ten we went to Whitstable for lunch with our best friends, Sunita and Chris, and to celebrate our first wedding anniversary. After the first course I went to the loo and discovered I was bleeding. My first urge was to try and stop the blood. Then I felt sick. Harry and I went outside and stood hugging on the shingle beach for a few minutes. Inside the restaurant, Sunita was in tears. If I'd been a diner I'd have been intrigued as to what was going on. We left immediately, driving back home in silence. We spent that evening quietly watching TV and drinking wine. I wondered if I'd known five days earlier that the embryos were leaving. What was wrong with them – or me?

It felt like a miscarriage but I'd never been pregnant. I had no right to mourn something that had never really existed; it strips you of a certain legitimacy. But the sense of loss was, again, overwhelming.

Over the following week we talked about what to do next. More strongly than ever, I felt we needed a Plan B. I couldn't go through it all again without my sights set further than the horizon. The chances of IVF ever working seemed so slim that I needed to try and come to terms with the possibility of us never having a child of our own. I wanted the treatment to be the back-up plan, not the main one. There were greater things for Harry and me out there; I just didn't know what they were, or how to find them.

A couple of weeks later we went to see our consultant, who suggested that we consider going elsewhere for treatment. It felt like a rejection. She thought we might have more success with another clinic that may have a different approach or perspective whereas with her, we'd go through exactly the same procedure – one that had already proved unsuccessful. We reluctantly agreed, and booked an appointment with a private clinic with a good reputation.

The laughs had been a bit thin on the ground but my relationship with Harry felt as strong as ever. Comrades-in-arms, it was us against the world. I'm sure we loved each other more after everything we'd been through. But that was before we went on holiday in May 1999 to Italy, a trip that has passed into our family folklore as the worst ever. We were staying in a house on the Tuscan / Umbrian border – a tall, narrow, gothic building that made us feel gloomy as soon as we stepped inside. Determined to enjoy myself, within the first five minutes I'd drawn up an itinerary of places to visit, which Harry immediately dismissed. He'd been to Italy once before on a disastrous holiday with an ex-girlfriend and didn't like it any better the second time around. I accused him of being narrow-minded; he accused me of being like my mother. It rained. We visited dark hill towns, peering out from the 'bella vista' spots through the mist. I'd always relied on Harry's enthusiasm but now when I looked at him he seemed so sad, so lost. We argued – I can't remember what about – and the atmosphere between us became as heavy and oppressive as the weather: I just wanted to go home. We visited Siena for the day to look at the frescos and the striped marble Duomo. Still our mood refused to lift. On the day we returned to London I sat under a tree at Rome airport and wept. The holiday had been hard. We didn't have the energy or lightness of spirit to shrug off bad weather and disappointing day trips, and felt an added layer of guilt and resentment that it hadn't been enjoyed as much as it should have been. As soon as we were back on home territory, we felt better. There were more distractions, and the routine of everyday life was reassuring.

* * *

I'd been immediately charmed by the fancy new clinic: there were no patients sitting outside with bandaged heads, having a fag, dragging their drips behind them. Inside the décor was sleek and slick, with silver-grey leather sofas in the waiting room and free tea and coffee making facilities. The nurses wore little pink uniforms cinched at the waist. Best of all were the statistics: they had a 44 per cent pregnancy success rate for women over the age of 35 undergoing ICSI – almost double that of our previous hospital.

That summer we got two kittens, so small they slept in Harry's sandals. A friend came to stay one night. 'Ah,' she said somewhat tactlessly after dinner, looking at the kittens purring on my lap, 'do they fulfil something in you?' I felt so patronised I nearly hit her. Instead I went to bed early.

I started the treatment that September feeling positive. The chaos theory slowly evolving over the past two years, which held that everything would end in disappointment, had been replaced by a far more upbeat, 'Why shouldn't we be the lucky ones?' attitude. It didn't last. On the day of the embryo transfer our appointment overran by an hour, during which time I sat in the waiting room desperate for a wee but unable to go – I'd been told I had to have a full bladder. The room also turned into a crèche when, for some reason, it filled with women and broods of children. When I finally went in for the procedure we were told that the three embryos being transferred were not particularly good-quality. 'Let's put it this way,' said the embryologist, 'it will be a miracle if you have twins.' The actual transfer was painful – I remember grunting a lot and halfway through, I had to get up and go to the loo. I'd wanted to wish the embryos well on their way, but instead I felt uncomfortable, disheartened and grumpy. Harry and I walked back to the car in silence. 'Poor blighters won't stand a chance with us mooching around like this,' I thought. I needed him to cheer me up, but he was going through his own misery.

The visualisation techniques that I'd tried the last time were all over the place. One minute I was imagining the embryos on a beanbag with velvet cushions, the next they were floating in bubble bath and blancmange. In the end I settled for the fishermen's cottages again. Harry and I spent a weekend on the North Norfolk coast, looking at the flat horizon and big skies, reassuring ourselves that somewhere there was a child out there for us, we just hadn't found each other yet.

On an overcast October morning, six weeks after I began treatment, my period started. Relieved, I couldn't even cry: it was finally all over. I couldn't bear the thought of being at home on my own, so I decided to go into work. I sat on the bus listening to my mini radio when Gil Scott-Heron's 'Your Daddy Loves You' came on. I knew if I cried I'd end up embarrassing everyone with loud, heaving sobs. Just at that moment I felt a tap on my shoulder and one of my sister's friends, an art director who I didn't know very well, sat down next to me. I tried to match his jolliness as we chatted about the fashion show he'd just worked on for Stella McCartney. That lunchtime I went out with a friend and drank two large glasses of wine. Finally, I cried.

A few weeks later we went back to have a chat with our old consultant, who confirmed to us that we'd reached the end of the line. She said she'd treat us again, but wouldn't encourage it. She backed up her argument with a statistic, saying we'd have something like an 11 per cent chance of success if we went through it all again. None of us thought it was worth it. I appreciated her honesty. The subject of adoption came up – had we thought about it? Harry said he'd consider it; I didn't feel ready.

There was a relief that came with drawing a line under the third cycle of treatment. We could have gone on – there are always new tests, different approaches, other people's sperm and eggs to try. But if we went down that path it might never end. A doctor at the clinic once told us proudly that one of his patients became pregnant after her seventeenth attempt. I realised I wasn't prepared to sacrifice my life in order to create a new one.

Over the next few months, from October onwards, I was busy and distracted. I went to Somalia with former Olympic swimmer Sharron Davies to cover her visit to an eye hospital working in the field. We flew from Kenya across Ethiopia in a ten-seater plane, landing on a patch of scrubland in the middle of nowhere, and stayed the night surrounded by armed guards. The following week I travelled to Lapland to cover a former soap-star-turned-pantomime-favourite meeting Santa Claus for a Christmas feature. The temperature was minus 30, so cold my eyelashes and nostril hairs froze. I saw the Aurora Borealis and at night in the hotel bar watched, transfixed, as respectable-looking Finns got so drunk, they collapsed on top of each other like dominos. The next weekend I went to Paris with my sister, where we shopped, ate and walked for hours around a cemetery. Harry, meanwhile, felt trapped at home, unable to escape. I could dip into a world that could be exciting without children, however briefly. But Harry was stuck in the same stomping ground, passing the hospital where we'd had treatment on an almost daily basis as he went about his business. We didn't argue about this, mainly because Harry, in a somewhat typical male way, kept his feelings to himself.

I found it exciting to have experiences outside the everyday, to remind myself how big the world was but inevitably my feelings caught up with me. With no more adventures to look forward to, I was hit by a wave of despondency and fear and couldn't distract myself from the same monotonous thought pattern: 'I have no plans, no goals'. The failed IVF treatments had taken away any sense of purpose and I felt a failure for not being able to find a fulfilling enough replacement. I wanted a consolation prize, for someone to say to me, 'Don't worry that you can't have your baby, have this lovely thing instead.'

At New Year we went to Norfolk with Sunita and Chris. They didn't have children, and it was a relief not to have to put on a 'brave face' or deal with a 'happy family' scenario. On the morning of New Year's Day, 2000, also Harry's birthday, we all got up at 7am and walked along the coastal sandbank to watch the sunrise. The sky was pink and flocks of geese flew noisily overhead. A perfectly round orange ball rose slowly from the horizon.

I felt a deep sadness, knowing I'd never have a child who looked like me, who shared my mannerisms or gestures. My family genes wouldn't be passed on. Harry and I would never nurture a child we'd made between us. Maybe we were meant to look after someone else's child, maybe he or she was out there somewhere, but for now I needed to grieve the loss of my own.

Chapter Two

I'm sitting in a semi-circle wearing a nametag in an over heated room. The group around me are shouting out a volley of expletives as I pray for the floor to swallow me up. Suddenly we're silenced with 'Turkey Diver' from an unassuming woman sitting at the back. What the hell was that? And what does it have to do with adoption?

Five months had passed since our final IVF attempt and I had started to feel cautiously optimistic about the future, which didn't look quite so hopeless. We'd just returned from a month's trip to Sri Lanka, where we visited ancient cities, temples and giant Buddhas and took part in a two-week yoga course on a white, sandy, palm-fringed beach with a group of strangers. Feeling slightly more in control, our conversation had turned to adoption. At this stage neither of us had particularly strong feelings about it either way but we were prepared to investigate. It gave us a plan, which helped muffle the profound sense of loss and grief we felt over our infertility: we were moving on to the next stage.

We'd taken a few tentative steps, making preliminary enquiries and approaching some adoption agencies run by local authorities, but so far with little success. One had already refused to meet us, saying there weren't any children on their books they could match with a white couple. At another we were left sitting in reception for half an hour after the social worker had forgotten about our meeting. Undaunted, we moved on. Even if our efforts so far had proved fruitless, at least it occupied us; it felt proactive. The thought of doing nothing at all was untenable.

It was a miserable February afternoon in 2000 when Harry and I had our first meeting with two social workers from a local authority. The room had the stuffy, municipal smell of an old school classroom, a mix of peeling paint and dust. The radiators were on full blast and the atmosphere was drowsy. In front of us sat Janice, a large, middle-aged, smiley woman with steely eyes and beaded earrings. To my right was Donna, stern-faced, with painted talons for nails. If they were trying to put us off, they were doing a good job.

We had friends who had adopted recently and so we knew it was a complex process. The climate was almost unrecognisable to 30-odd years earlier when single women would be shamed into giving up their babies born out of wedlock, and childless couples could take their pick. Children up for adoption now have more than likely been taken away from their birth parents rather than relinquished by them, and come through the care system. Many would have had a troubled family history, including drug or drink addiction, abuse or neglect. Taking on one of these children is a very different experience to adopting a newborn. Attitudes within the adoption world to potential adopters had also changed over the years. Their needs were no longer the priority – it was a matter of finding the right parents for the child, not the right child for the parents. I hadn't as yet taken any of this on board. My main concern at this stage was: could I love a child that wasn't my own?

But of course it wasn't as easy as that, as Janice and Donna were quick to point out. Maybe they were trying to sort out the wheat from the chaff – there were still far more people wanting to adopt healthy babies than there were healthy babies available. Some sort of elimination process was necessary. They used shock tactics. First, we were shown a list of potential 'issues' that could affect a child and asked which we'd be prepared to consider. What level of mental or physical disability? How about behavioural problems? Could we cope with a child that had been consistently sexually abused? How did we feel about learning difficulties? A 'normal' baby clearly wasn't an option. When the subject of schizophrenia came up, I said I didn't think I'd be able to deal with it. At this Donna threw me a dirty look. 'The illness can be very easily treated with drugs these days,' she snapped. Nor did it go down well when I admitted that if pushed, I thought I'd cope better with a physical rather than mental disability. Janice then launched into a well-honed lecture about each child bringing his own 'little suitcase of problems' with him.

'Truck-load, more like,' I thought.

Knowing the unlikelihood of adopting a baby we'd decided that we would consider children up to the age of two. Immediately we were asked if we'd go up to four. By this stage Harry and I were playing good cop/bad cop, with me being all, 'No, we couldn't possibly', which he'd modify with, 'Well, we wouldn't rule it out.' It wasn't that we disagreed with each other; we both knew what we felt we were able to cope with. It was just that when put under pressure, Harry tended to be conciliatory while I was more combative. However, I still felt guilty, confused and compromised by their questions. The message was loud and clear: the child was the priority and our needs and concerns came second. Which is exactly how it should be; except as a potential adopter, it made me feel at best selfish and heartless, and at worst a criminal.

We left two-and-a-half hours later, feeling slightly hysterical and joking that we'd end up with an eight-year-old with a drug problem and a criminal record. The picture that had been presented to us was so unremittingly bleak and joyless that I couldn't help but think we'd just been put through a test to see if we would return.

Despite the ease with which I seemed to say the 'wrong' thing, we were invited back for a weekend group 'preparation' course, in which we'd learn about the ins and outs of the adoption process. By now I was gripped by a dogged determination: I needed to find out if the prospect of adoption really was that grim or whether it could offer us a happy family life. On an intellectual level, I'd also become engaged in the subject – it had opened up a world I'd known nothing about and I was curious to discover more. It was a puzzle I had to solve; a mission I must complete.

A few weeks later we were sitting in that same room

again, sipping coffee and nibbling biscuits with around 16 people, mainly couples. I had nothing in common with any of them. This was based on purely superficial observations – they looked like sensible, sorted, middle England types who read the *Daily Mail* and keep a Mondeo in the garage. But one thing united us: our desire to have a child. Over the next three days we were given a crash course by three social workers, including our friend Janice, on adoption issues, starting with loss. This, we were told, was the cornerstone of adoption, with all parties suffering – the birth parents for losing their child, the child for being separated from his birth parents and the adoptive parents for not having their own biological child. It was a triangle of grief upon which adoptive families had to build.

After a politically correct lunch of rice, beans and plantain, we sat back down for a chat about child development. The little suitcase of problems made a re-appearance to demonstrate how early traumatic events in a child's life, such as neglect or abuse, could affect his or her developmental milestones. We were given photocopied papers written by paediatricians and child psychologists on clinical testing procedures and developmental progress for children at different ages. I felt blinded by science. We were then tested on our own knowledge of what was done at what stage. Would a three-year-old dance to music? 'Without a doubt,' I said. 'Not necessarily,' I was told. I felt ignorant, then resentful: why should I know anything about a child's intellectual or physical development? Anyone expecting his or her first child wouldn't have a clue either.

I wasn't sure whether this was a rather cruel, pointless exercise or a demonstration in how we had to modify our expectations. The discussion became even more worrying when it turned to regression. Many children taken from their birth families and brought up in care would have missed out on the essential nurturing and security they needed as babies, and might well want to regress to that lost age. It was fine, indeed it should be encouraged, if an eight-year-old wanted to wear a nappy in bed or drink milk from a bottle. But this wasn't something I could see myself being able to embrace.

The day ended with a discussion about swearing – some of the children, we were told, would have a good line in rude words. We were asked to shout out all the ones we could think of as 'F***', 'C***' and 'W*****' – and 'Turkey Diver' – were written up on the flip chart. Maybe they were trying to test our shockability, but it felt ridiculous.

That night we drank more wine than was wise and returned to the course the following morning hungover and with that 'back-to-school' feeling. The day kicked off with a discussion about behavioural problems, from children smearing faeces on the wall to watching too much TV. We were told that children who had been sexually abused might have overtly sexualised behaviour, as it was the only way they knew how to receive affection or to communicate with adults. We sat quietly, trying to digest the difficult facts. With time, love and patience, the problems would apparently become less severe. When I suggested that some of these kids might be so damaged they would never heal, that they needed more than just a little TLC, the social workers' covert glances felt disapproving. In the tea break I was reassured by one of them that they welcomed the discussion being opened up with questions, but there seemed to be no room for doubt or negativity.

Or secrecy. In part a reaction to the culture of concealment that once prevailed, when many children weren't told of their adoption – or not until they were adults – a culture of openness was now encouraged. Children not only needed to know that they were adopted, but they needed to know the circumstances, however unsettling. There were no skeletons in closets or stones left unturned. A man in my discussion group said he'd rather keep sexual abuse quiet – that sometimes it was better not to know these things. It was as if an elephant had just walked into the room. Again, nothing was said, but it felt as though his card had been marked.

'Isn't it strange,' I thought – looking around at everyone in the room, with their notepads and their enthusiasm – 'that all of us here who are unable to have our own children have to not only jump through hoops but consider kids we may never come into contact with, and situations we'd ordinarily go to some length to avoid. Do the infertile end up with the damaged goods?'

The day ended with a visit from a single mother who had an eight-year-old adopted son. She told us how, on the three-hour train journey down to meet us, she had been trying to persuade him to leave the toilet in which he had barricaded himself. Once out, he had kicked, screamed and punched her. Apparently this wasn't unusual behaviour. Since she had adopted two years ago she had given up her career and moved house to look after him. She looked drained and beaten but she said she hadn't regretted a minute of it. I couldn't understand why, except to assume that she was made of sterner stuff than me.

By the end of the course I could think and talk of nothing else but it was almost impossible to explain our experience to other people. Both Harry and I felt as if we'd entered a strange world that we were still trying to understand ourselves. When I attempted to explain it to my mum she looked worried, saying she wanted a chat with me, 'mother to daughter'. But in the end she held back. Whatever she was going to advise, she wanted me to discover for myself.

The course had fascinated but scared me. I feared I wasn't capable of taking on the challenges described but something kept drawing me back. Maybe it was arrogance: I knew, or assumed, that we wouldn't have a child whose problems were so severe that we wouldn't be able to cope or look after them properly. We wanted to be parents, not social workers. Somewhere, still lurking in the shadows, was the child of our dreams. We just didn't know where to find him or her. But I was beginning to doubt it would be in Britain.

We'd already talked about the possibility of looking for a child abroad and the idea was beginning to take shape. International adoption had been touched on in the preparation meetings, though not in a positive way. It seemed to be frowned upon by the social services, who appeared keener for people to adopt from Britain than to seek children from other countries. But there were genuine concerns to consider. Although there were more babies available abroad than in the UK – especially from countries such as China – many of them would have been abandoned. This, naturally, could have a significant psychological impact later in life as not only would a child feel an acute sense of rejection, tracing his or her birth family would be almost impossible. There could be large gaps in the child's history, leaving huge question marks over his health, both mental and physical. There was also the question of identity: taking a child away from his own country was stripping him of its culture. In some quarters this was considered tantamount to abuse. (Around the same time as investigating international adoption I heard a discussion on the radio in which the head of one London local authority – who clearly held some pretty radical beliefs – said it was better for a child to die on the streets in poverty than to be taken away from his native country. That made me angry.) Finally, race was obviously an issue – an 'average' white couple might encounter racism with a child of Asian, African or Latin American descent and not necessarily be equipped to deal with it.

And yet, international adoption seemed so much more romantic; glamorous too. Angelina Jolie and Brad Pitt weren't yet making headlines with their 'rainbow family' but it's easy to see why they've captured the world's imagination: a beautiful actress, together with her handsome actor-producer husband, adopt children from developing countries around the world to give them a better life. Jolie's work as a goodwill ambassador for the UN refugee agency makes her actions seem all the more genuine. The couple have presented an image of racial harmony as well as unity between their birth children and those they have adopted. Whether we're being presented with a fantasy or a positive reflection of family life, the Jolie-Pitt set-up encapsulates the allure of foreign adoption as altruistic and exciting and, if you have the time and resources, a bit of a no-brainer, which was what appealed to me. Madonna has fared less well, perhaps because her adoption of two children from Malawi has brought into sharp focus some of the more negative aspects of international adoption, with accusations of rule-bending, fast-tracking and apparent discord with the children's relatives. And yet both these celebrity examples tap into the powerfully seductive 'prince and pauper' fairytale.

It was around this time that my 'Pros and Cons' lists began to appear. The first was for British adoption, with the cons far outweighing the pros. I still have the piece of paper. 'Child's difficult behaviour so severe that our world disappears,' reads one point. 'Ongoing contact with birth family = resentment/fear,' reads another.

I was writing my way out of it.

I am, by nature, a nosey person and have found the best way to gather information is by speaking to other people. Professionally, I could use this to my advantage. As a journalist working for women's magazines, I knew that adoption, particularly international adoption, had all the components of a fascinating story, so I started to do some research. The more I looked into it, the more it appealed.

I'd first heard Claire talking about her extraordinary family on BBC Radio 4 a year earlier, and managed to track her down for an interview. I spent several hours at her large London home listening to her experiences of adopting three children from three different countries in Latin America. It was a fascinating evening. 'I didn't expect to adore them the minute I set eyes on them,' she told me. 'I just had a sense that love would grow.'

When he was five years old, her son Benedict (now 13), whom she'd adopted from El Salvador as a baby, told his parents that a piece of him was missing and that he needed to find his birth mother. After a year's search they found his mother, Gloria, living in a town outside San Salvador with her three other sons. Together, Claire and Benedict flew out to meet her. After that meeting, the family continued to stay in touch and made regular visits to El Salvador. Benedict, who now has a relationship with both his mothers, told me he felt whole: 'I'd lost a piece, and then I found it again and completed the puzzle.'

It wasn't only Claire's courage that impressed me – could I have flown across the other side of the world to meet my son's mother? But also her selflessness. 'I've never looked upon them as possessions,' she said of her children. 'I've always felt that I was given them to look after, and that they were never my property. I've just borrowed them.' The sentiment resonated with me. There was something about adoption that took away any sense of parental 'ownership', which I quite liked. Although I think, conversely, it was linked to a fear that I might feel the child didn't belong to me, that I wasn't its 'proper' mother. International adoption took that one step further – the fact that your child came from another country and culture reinforced that divide. And in an odd sort of way it made sense.

In comparison to the few examples of domestic adoption we'd come across so far, the stories I heard about overseas adoption were joyful and optimistic. 'When I wake up, I'm excited because the first thing I see is her,' Carmel, a single mother who had adopted her baby daughter from China, told me in another interview. 'This was meant to be; we were made for each other, and that was something I hadn't expected – this sense of destiny.'

With such potent, emotive accounts, I couldn't help but feel fired up. I didn't have to think about drug-addled mums with feral kids from desperate estates, who lived a stone's throw away. Poverty abroad – the crucial factor in most overseas adoption – was unfamiliar, far away and difficult to imagine. I was happy to look through double-glazed, rose-tinted spectacles.

We started to make our own investigations into adopting internationally. Harry had spent a few years living in Costa Rica and Nicaragua so it made sense to look into Latin America. China also seemed like a sensible choice – not least because its one-child policy at the time meant that countless babies were still being left abandoned. Children, particularly girls, were in need of families because of a brutal political system, not because of the demands and needs of childless Westerners. No one could question the moral or ethical integrity of bringing home a child from China but I felt no real passion or interest for the country or culture, something I felt I'd have to have were we to adopt from there.

Naturally, the process was a bureaucratic nightmare. Anyone who wants to adopt from abroad still has to go through a homestudy – the lengthy assessment that all adoptive parents are put through by social services – but unlike domestic adoption, you have to pay – at the time it was around £2,000. To make matters more complicated, adoptions from some countries aren't legally recognised in Britain, so another adoption procedure must be completed on return to the UK.

Small matters, we thought. I began searching the internet, looking at the websites of different adoption agencies in Latin America. Many of them were geared to an American market – pictures of cute, plump kids with round faces and bright eyes, with endearing, upbeat messages. As I made contact with people around the world who were adopting from Guatemala, receiving emails from Cornwall to Connecticut, I felt part of a global network.

'You'll discover there are a lot of people out there who don't think the same way as you,' wrote one. 'There are a few people in positions of influence who vehemently disagree with inter-country adoption and spend a lot of time publicising their cause. You just have to keep trying to focus on the positive – that you are going to adopt a child that otherwise would not have had much of a life staying behind in an institution in their own country.'

The downside was the finance: foreign adoption is an expensive business. With many countries in Latin America you have to go through an American-based agency and pay a lawyer astronomical fees. We estimated it would cost us at least £20,000, which we didn't have. Then again, some people spend that on a new kitchen but the financial transaction made us feel uncomfortable. Someone, somewhere, was making a handsome profit from other people's misery.

I felt like a seasoned preparation groupie when we trudged along to yet another meeting, this time about overseas adoption. It was all very civilised – for completely superficial reasons. There was a more eclectic group of people; the visiting adoptive parents were far more inspiring. And the biscuits were tastier. But that was before I became Public Enemy Number One with the Guatemalan Families Association, when it all went a bit pear-shaped...

I had emailed its secretary, informing her of our interest in adopting from Guatemala, and also to ask if any of their members would be interviewed for a feature I was writing. Her response knocked me sideways as she accused me of putting my journalistic concerns above my adoption interests. She told me I was in no position to write about the subject until I'd had the experience of being an adoptive mother; that she wasn't going to put forward any of her members as 'fodder' for my article and that it would probably jeopardise my chances of getting through a homestudy if the social services ever got wind of what I was writing about. I was furious and hurt; I was on their side – why the anger? Other members of the organisation I'd been in touch with reassured me, explaining Guatemala had become a happy hunting ground for journalists looking for a 'baby-snatching' scandal and that the secretary had recently had a bad experience with a somewhat unscrupulous documentary maker. Paranoia was rife and she had to be on her guard to protect those who had legitimately, and successfully, adopted children and built happy family lives. Her mistrust was understandable. A few days later a full-page article appeared in the *Guardian* about a UN report on adoption abuses in Guatemala. According to another article, many adoptions from there were legitimate, but allegedly there was growing evidence to suggest a significant number of children had been 'bought' illegally.

It made for sombre reading, which wasn't helped by the fact that around the same time we had a reply from one of the American-based adoption agencies. We were told we'd have to have an interview (in London), which would cost us $2,350 (£1,500) for the privilege.

I didn't know what to think, or who to talk to. No one could offer us impartial, objective advice. We seemed to be considering options that were ripe for exploitation – vulnerable mothers, their babies and childless couples, all of them desperate. I didn't want to be part of anything where there was even a whiff of corruption. Where once I'd felt hope, now I felt confusion, again.

That summer Harry and I went on a week's yoga holiday in Southern Spain, where we did nothing except practice yoga, eat healthy food, swim, walk and talk. For the first time in two years we began to consider a life that didn't include children. I thought about yoga and the possibilities of teaching it. We talked about buying a place in Spain and possibly living there; we didn't discuss children at all. And when we did, eventually, we wondered if we could do all these things *and* have a family. How could we downshift, change careers, move country, if we had to support a child? We had never seriously considered any of these options before; we'd been too busy pursuing the one thing we couldn't have.

My ability to make a decision had deserted me. In six months we had considered everything from what felt like the bleakness of domestic adoption and the potential exploitation of overseas adoption to the liberating but terrifying prospect of childlessness. We could move to Spain, change careers, travel the world, write novels... There would just be a big hole in my heart.

And so it continued. Despite all our brave talk we couldn't let go. We weren't yet ready to give up the dream of having a child. A few weeks later we made another appointment to talk to yet another social worker – this time from an independent adoption agency, Childlink (which later became PACT – Parents and Children Together). And it was refreshingly positive. We were told not only were there plenty of younger children and babies in Britain to adopt – the trend had recently shifted in social services from being anti- to pro-adoption – but also attitudes were changing towards placing mixed-heritage and black children with white parents. Previously, this had always been a non-starter. As an independent agency, Childlink wouldn't force us to consider any child we didn't want to – they were on our side.

We'd explored every avenue, and there was nothing left to investigate. We just had to answer the basic questions: were we prepared for how adoption might affect the rest of our lives; were we about to make a huge mistake or would we never look back?

It was then that I was blindsided after a visit to my friend Ruth. In April she had given birth to a son, Louis. Now six months old, he was a firm, beautiful, cuddly baby. One warm August afternoon I visited, determined to keep a grip and enjoy it, which I did. I sat in the garden with Louis on my lap; I fed him his bottle and tickled him in his carrycot. As I kissed his cheeks, I breathed in his baby smell. Ruth and I watched as he napped on a blanket in the sun. He made Ruth feel happy and whole; he made me feel empty and sad. Louis proved quite instrumental in our adoption process. We bonded as he grew into a delightful toddler, and often we'd 'borrow' him for afternoons in the park, to practise our child management skills. He made us feel confident about our potential to become parents.

But that day I cried when I got home. Why couldn't something so fundamentally simple, natural and *right* be ours? What would *our* baby have been like? A composite of us, someone in whom I'd look for traces of Harry and me; a continuation of us, he would complete us. Ruth had asked me if I'd given up all hope of it ever happening, and I'd said yes, I had to.

But I wasn't ready for what felt, at the time, to be the consolation prize of adoption. How could I love someone else's child when I was still coming to terms with the loss of my own?

I couldn't go any further until I'd put that one to rest.

Chapter Three

O ur adoption story isn't the first in my family, something I only properly realised when I started writing
this book.

My late dad, Syd, who was born in 1930, grew up the
youngest of four children in a poor, working-class family
in Battersea, south London. An unplanned child, there
was a ten-year age gap between him and his next, older
sibling. When she was 17, his eldest sister, Alice, who
wasn't married, fell pregnant and had a daughter, Marge.
One day, the story goes, she was standing in the local fish
and chip shop when the owner said, 'That's a lovely baby,'
to which Alice replied: 'Would you like to buy her?'

It was a serious question, and had they said yes, Alice
would have handed her daughter over to the care of the
fish and chip shop owners. But no money changed hands.
Instead, Marge was taken in by my grandmother and
brought up as my dad's sister. With just a five-year age
gap between uncle and niece, they formed a close bond.

Marge, who was extremely bright, won a place at grammar school, where a teacher recognised her potential and offered to bring her up in a less impoverished environment, both materially and intellectually. She eventually married a professor and emigrated to Canada.

While it may not be a traditional adoption story, the extraordinary chain of events that saw Marge move from a series of households and carers is typical of the casual exchange of children that once happened so easily and without intervention from either the law or the social services.

According to Dr Jenny Keating, a senior research fellow at the Institute of Historical Research, the practice in the 1930s of handing over children to complete strangers, or to other members of the extended family, wasn't uncommon. 'There are no numbers, but anecdotally [we know] it happened,' she tells me. 'Doctors and nurses would do it too. An unmarried woman could say to her GP, "Look, I'm pregnant, do you know anyone who wants to have a baby?" and he'd say, "Oh, that's funny, because Mrs so-and-so down the road is desperate." They could then either have the baby officially adopted, or it could all be done informally.'

* * *

In the last 100 years, we've evolved from a completely unlegislated, casual and often cruel system of adoption to a tightly controlled, highly legislated procedure aiming to put the welfare of the child at its centre. We've moved on from the stigma of illegitimacy and a culture of secrecy and shame to one of openness and accountability.

Adoption is no longer about finding healthy babies for childless couples but finding parents for some of our most vulnerable children.

Having gone through the process and come out the other side, I wanted to find out how adoption has evolved, why over the past few decades it's gone in and out of favour and what the social attitudes are that have shaped it. How do we legislate and control such a highly emotive and complex process? I'm not an historian or academic but I've tried to get to grips with as much as I can about the birth and development of a system that gave us our son.

* * *

One of my first ports of call in researching this chapter was to visit The Foundling Museum in central London. Often we'd take Gabriel to play at Coram's Fields, a playground and park dedicated to children on the site of the former old hospital, which was established by a philanthropic sea captain, Thomas Coram, in 1739 for the 'education and maintenance of exposed and deserted young children'.

I had arranged to meet the museum's curator, Stephanie Chapman, in its café, where the walls are inscribed with figures from literature who have been adopted or fostered – from Heathcliff to Harry Potter, Superman, James Bond, Jane Eyre, Frodo Baggins and Princess Leia. I found it strangely moving, these characters revealed in a new light.

Coram founded the hospital when, after years of living in the American colonies, on his return to London in 1720 he was shocked by the number of babies he saw left for dead or abandoned on the city streets. 'He thought it was a cruel and horrific waste of life and felt that babies could be turned into useful citizens,' explains Chapman.

After a seventeen-year campaign to raise money, the hospital (which meant 'hospitality' or home in the traditional sense of the word) first opened its doors to children in 1741. Coram knew many of the musicians and artists of the time, including Handel, who arranged special performances of The Messiah there and William Hogarth, who donated pictures to raise funds. Despite there being a strong philanthropic movement at the time, people feared it would become an easy way to get rid of illegitimate children, 'and might encourage licentiousness, or for men to take advantage of young women,' says Chapman, hence Coram's long struggle to raise funds.

To avoid being accused of encouraging immorality, the hospital would only take the woman's first child – any subsequent children would not be accepted.

'On the very first day of admissions, it was noted that the cries of the women leaving their children were as upsetting as the cries of the women whose children weren't accepted,' says Chapman.

In the 19th century – and in keeping with Victorian moral standards – focus shifted to the character of the mother, who had to come from what was considered a 'respectable' background – that is, a hard worker who had fallen from grace but was able to return to work once the hospital had taken her child. Babies were usually around a month old when they were taken in and immediately sent out to a wet nurse, where they were fostered. At five years old, they returned to live at the hospital until they were apprenticed out, sometimes as young as nine years old – the boys to the Navy and the girls into domestic service.

Children would be stripped of their name and given another as soon as they entered, so the mother left a token with the child's papers so that she could identify her child should she ever return to reclaim him or her – a practice that wasn't encouraged. Some of these keepsakes, ranging from jewellery to buttons, enamel badges, pearl hearts, hairclips and ribbons, are on display in the museum, along with heartbreaking messages written for the child – 'You have my heart, though we must part', 'Go gentle babe'. Over time, the tokens were replaced by receipts, for the simple fact that if a mother were accused of infanticide she could prove she hadn't killed her child but had left him or her in the safe care of the hospital.

The children were clothed, fed, given excellent medical care and taught a trade but were severely lacking in emotional care and were bullied, stigmatised and often traumatised after returning to an institution having lived in a foster home for the first few years of their lives. But what we would consider cruel by modern standards, however, was seen as remarkable at the time, says Chapman: 'It was the first ever children's charity and it was groundbreaking. When the hospital closed in the 1950s, institutional care was very out-of-date and behind the times but when it started it was a really innovative solution to a problem, and ahead of its time, when infant mortality stood at 90 per cent and many of these children would have died in the workhouse.'

The legacy it left was significant: the work first started by Thomas Coram 275 years ago today continues with the children's charity Coram, one of the UK's leading adoption agencies.

* * *

At the turn of the 20th century life was relentlessly harsh for any single woman who had a child. Both were considered shameful by society – the mother for having transgressed a strict moral code by having sex outside marriage, and the illegitimate child for inheriting her 'bad blood'. If working in domestic service, a single mother was more than likely to be dismissed. If forced into a workhouse, she would often be discriminated against. The very few homes for mothers and babies were equally harsh and judgemental. In desperation, babies were often abandoned, sold or even murdered. Baby farming – the practice of giving illegitimate babies to unscrupulous people who 'adopted' them to sell or dispose of them – was not uncommon.

Adoption wasn't legally recognised in Britain until 1926, but in the First World War it became more organised. Up until then (and even after it became legislated) adoptions were arranged informally and privately: neighbours taking in local children, extended family members helping out, or occasionally babies were given to people unknown to the family, with money changing hands.

The arrival of the First World War, however, saw a growing call for legislation, for pragmatic reasons. 'There was a rise in orphaned children and illegitimate children, with women having fleeting romances with men coming back from the Front and then going off again, women getting engaged and then pregnant, only for their fiancé to get killed,' says Dr Keating, whose book, *A Child for*

Keeps, traces the history of adoption in England up to 1945. By the end of the War in 1918, there were a record 42,000 illegitimate births – with unmarried mothers having to deal not just with the shame but also the practical difficulties of surviving on their own without income, childcare or often anywhere to live.

At the same time, a number of adoption agencies run by volunteers had sprung up, aimed at matching people who wanted a family with mainly illegitimate children and orphans. Adoption was beginning to be considered, by these agencies at least, as a solution to homeless children and childless couples. It was as far away from the 'triangle of loss' - the birth parents for losing their child – the child for being separated from his birth parents and the adoptive parents for not having their own biological child – which is acknowledged today in adoption, as you can get.

'It would have been seen in completely different terms,' explains Dr Keating. 'The birth mother would get a chance to start again – she'd made a mistake, got pregnant, and now she could have a clean slate. The child would get a whole new life and family, and the childless parents would get a child.'

Throughout the 1920s these agencies pushed for adoption to be legalised and for regulation on a practice that was so open to abuse. After much to-ing and fro-ing, an Act was eventually passed in 1926, which, although basic, made adoption legally binding. However, there was no proper regulation of the adoption agencies or thorough vetting of potential adopters. The Act wasn't even compulsory – a child could still be taken in by another family and not even be registered as adopted.

With adoption now legal and on the road to respectability, the number of adoptions steadily rose from 3,000 children in 1927, the year after the Adoption of Children Act came into force, to over 5,000 by 1936. Secrecy prevailed, upheld by agencies for fear they might discourage what they described as a 'better' sort of adopter if everything was out in the open, and by adopting parents, most of whom were married, infertile couples.

'It was because of the stigma of adopting an illegitimate child,' explains Dr Keating. 'If you suddenly popped up with a child and your neighbours knew you hadn't been pregnant, they would guess you'd adopted. So people moved around the country. There was also a stigma around infertility as well,' she adds. '[It was considered] as [being] something wrong with your family.'

* * *

David Waller was adopted in 1938 when he was eight months old and carried the burden of secrecy throughout his childhood and into adulthood. An only child who grew up in Oxfordshire, he was never told his background by his adopted parents.

'Looking back now, there were lots of moments when I should have questioned things,' says David, 77, whose story was one of the most poignant I came across during my research. 'There'd be comments like, "I'll take you back to where you came from". My grandmother would say, "Don't take any notice of him – he's not one of us."'

It wasn't until he was nine years old that David discovered the truth, when he overheard a couple of friends talking about him at school. 'I grabbed my best friend and asked what they'd been saying, and he just came out and said, "You're adopted."

'That moment changed my whole life. I felt like an outcast,' he says. 'I withdrew into a shell.'

Both mother and son remained complicit in their secrecy, neither of them acknowledging or discussing the fact that he was adopted, right up until his mother's death, aged 101.

'I was too distraught, too upset that she wasn't my mother. I'm not blaming her: it was me, I withdrew from her. She noticed, probably, but nothing was ever said.'

Although he suspects everyone in the community knew that he was adopted, growing up he didn't tell anyone else – 'It was a secret I carried with me.' Instead he tried to uncover what he could, rifling through drawers and looking for evidence until eventually he found a birth certificate with his mother's name, father unknown, and his date and place of birth.

In the 1990s, David began to trace his birth family (without his adoptive mother's knowledge) and discovered that he'd been born in a home for 'wayward women' where, at 23 years old and unmarried, his mother, Mabel, had stayed. Two years later, she married and had another son whom she also called David, who died at 17. He was told this by a cousin, whose first words to him when they met were: 'You've got the Griffiths' nose – you're Mabel's son.'

He also met his mother's best friend, who told him: 'Your mother never said a word [about you]. The closest she ever came to it was when David died. She was in floods of tears and said, "I lost another one at six months."'

Discovering this information about his birth mother and

meeting his cousin gave David, 'A great sense of peace. It felt as if a burden had been lifted from my shoulders. It also changed my relationship with my adopted mum – I felt more at peace with her.'

But the stigma that surrounded his upbringing has been a constant source of sadness for David, despite being happily married to Myrtle for many years and having three children and six grandchildren, with whom he enjoys a close and open relationship.

'I've hidden so much. I would have been able to have a more open relationship with my mother, and I think she would have been a happier person too. You put something in the background and it's like a cancer that grows.'

* * *

Despite the legalisation of adoption in 1926, informal adoptions within the family or with 'compassionate' (or not so compassionate) strangers were still the norm. Largely unvetted, adoption agencies were left to their own devices, with some suspected of less than rigorous checks on potential adopters. The issue raised its head again, with newspaper reports appearing throughout the 1930s about 'bad' adoptions, of children being taken in and used as unpaid servants, or being shipped overseas to America or the Netherlands.

In 1939, a new Adoption Act put adoption agencies under the regulation of local authorities. Advertising – whether it was a parent putting up a child for adoption, a potential adopter wanting a child or anyone arranging adoptions – was made illegal. Potential adopters now had to be assessed (acknowledging for the first time the child's interests) and the local authority informed of any child adopted informally (i.e. not through an agency) under the age of nine.

With these new measures, adoption began to evolve from an entirely informal practice, with little legal protection, to becoming a reasonably regulated process that ensured potential adopters were capable and committed. However, it wasn't implemented until 1943 owing to the Second World War, which began just as it passed into legislation.

As with the First World War, the Second World War brought with it another peak in illegitimate births and a considerable rise in the number of adoptions, with over 21,000 in 1946. Every time a report appeared on war orphans, adoption agencies were flooded by requests for children – especially girls. However, scandals continued throughout the War, says Dr Keating, with, 'lots of stories of people passing children over on railway platforms.'

Although figures are hard to come by, there is plenty of anecdotal evidence, writes Keating in her book, of married women having babies by other men while their husbands were away at service. Although some children were accepted into the family by returning husbands, many more were adopted. Novelist and screenwriter Ian McEwan's mother, for example, had a baby boy by another man while her husband was serving overseas and having placed an advertisement in the local paper, gave the child away to a couple on Reading station.

Adoption agencies and organisations were now controlled, but private adoptions were still common. Friends, acquaintances or professionals in regular contact with unmarried mothers, including doctors, nurses, matrons in maternity homes and solicitors were often involved in arranging adoptions privately.

In 1950, a new Adoption Act consolidated legislation, tightened up the rules and introduced the 'clean break' nature of adoption, whereby adopters were not to be identified. Instead serial numbers were used in place of names on adoption records, protecting their anonymity.

By the 1950s there was a marked shift in the public perception of adoption. What was once considered a simple answer to the problem of illegitimacy was now a potential solution for childless couples with fertility problems. It was no longer a case of finding a home for an unwanted baby, but finding a 'real home with a real mother and father for a much wanted child' as it was put in one Government report of the time. Great efforts were also made to match children to parents in terms of looks, social background and even supposed intellectual potential to create a family as close to a biological one as possible.

Important advances in child development were also being made. The idea that nurture could have just as great an impact, if not more so, than nature in guiding a child's physical and intellectual potential was gaining ground. The belief that 'bad blood' could pass from mother to child had been a strong one but new scientific theories gave hope to the idea that you could beat nature by giving your child the best physical, emotional and intellectual environment.

With the increased numbers of 'unwanted' babies following the War, the improving reputation of adoption agencies and the growing acceptability to the middle classes, the elements were in place for adoption to enter its boom years of the 1950s and 1960s.

* * *

These two decades were characterised by what could be described as 'classic' adoption practice – the majority of children were under two years old, illegitimate and adopted by childless couples and placed by adoption societies. The children were considered 'adoptable' for being white, newborn and healthy.

In 1968, adoption reached its peak, when almost 25,000 Adoption Orders were made, thus severing the ties between birth parent and child, and handing over full parental responsibility for the child, to the approved adopters. The figures have never been so high since. But not all were relinquished babies: 35 per cent of all children were adopted by their own parents (often jointly with a new partner) or in order to legitimise the child of a single parent.

The continued stigma of illegitimacy meant that unmarried mothers were still vilified. On a practical level life was made difficult for them – private landlords discriminated against single women with children, there was little council housing available and women with children were often exploited by employers. The punitive voice of the religious moralisers preaching about sin and punishment was strong.

So if an unmarried mother still desperately wanted to keep her baby – and many of them did – society made it difficult for her to do so. 'The argument put by the adoption society to the unmarried mother was that even if she could manage to look after her child, adoptive families could give it a much better deal in life,' Dr Keating explains.

In recent years there's been a small but growing group of women who argue that adoption practice at the time was highly flawed and that many women were coerced into handing over their babies to be adopted. The Movement for an Adoption Apology, set up in 2010, is seeking a public apology from the British Government for women who were 'coerced, cajoled and conned' into giving up their babies.

Some single, pregnant women went to mother and baby homes run by the Church or adoption societies, often six weeks before they were due to give birth (to hide them from neighbours and relatives) until six weeks afterwards, the statutory minimum time allowed before consent for adoption could be given.

Helen Townsend's mother gave birth to her at St Faith's mother and baby home in Maidstone, Kent, on 3rd September 1968 – one of 25,000 babies adopted that year. 'My birth mother was 16, and so was my birth father, apparently,' she tells me. 'On my original birth certificate it says she's from Stroud, so they sent her there to have me.'

Helen's story is both commonplace and extraordinary. The mother of three children between the ages of 23 and eight years old, she is accepting and apparently nonplussed about her adoption. What I find astonishing, however, is the network of adopted people she has around her. Together, they represent the adoption boom years of the 1960s. Her husband, Andi, was adopted in 1963, 18 months after his adopted sister. Helen also had an older brother who was adopted (who died when he was 40) and a friend at school – who remains her best friend – with an adopted sister.

'There were four of us when I was growing up, but since then I've met quite a few other people who were adopted, and then I married someone who was as well, which raised a few eyebrows,' laughs Helen. 'My mum always said, "I'll tell you everything I know," which she did as we were growing up, so it was never a secret. It was just normal, and because there were quite a few of us, I never felt different.'

Their shared background has, Helen and Andi believe, made them closer.

'I probably identified more strongly with her,' says Andi, who first met Helen in 1991. 'But because I'm so easy with my adoption it's never surprised me when other people tell me they are.'

Andi, who works in IT at a school, was born in Watford and adopted when he was around two months old. He has no other details and no interest in knowing any either.

'I wasn't even curious to find out anything about my birth parents. If somebody said they were looking to find out who I was, I wouldn't have any qualms about them making contact, but I've never felt the need to dig up the information. What you don't know doesn't hurt you but if you open up a whole can of worms there could be a lot of things you don't want to find out,' he says.

'I've heard [other adopted people] say, "Is it because they didn't want me?" But in my mind, there was obviously a good reason behind the decision to have your child adopted, especially back when we were born. They were either giving you up to give you a better life or the stigma of not being married meant that they had to.'

Helen, who grew up with adoptive parents who loved her 'to bits', was equally uninterested in finding out more about her birth mother, until she had her own children.

'Everyone kept saying to me, "They look so much like you," so I started to wonder, "Do I look like my birth mother?"

'I wouldn't mind tracing her, even if it's only to get a photograph to see what she looks like. I don't want a relationship with her – it's far too late for that,' she adds. 'I'm curious, more than anything.'

She often wondered, even while growing up, what it must have been like for her 16-year-old mother to give up her baby: 'It must have been one of the hardest things she could have done. I don't know how she must have felt. I can only imagine it was a position she was put in and that it was the only outcome.'

Helen remembers her mum telling her brother that his birth mother didn't want to give him up, but was forced to because his birth father was a married man. She sent him clothes and blankets to take home with him to his new, adoptive family. 'I always remember my brother saying, "She should have fought harder for me," which upset my mum. He looked for her on and off throughout his life, but more seriously towards the end, but passed away before he had the chance to find her. He struggled with [his adoption] far more than I ever did.

'I think I was in a better place because my birth mum didn't want me,' she adds. 'But I was always happy with my mum and dad.'

* * *

By the end of the 1960s, the social climate had changed substantially and with it the whole face of adoption. Abortion became legal in 1967 and the oral contraceptive pill became widely available to single women – marriage was no longer a prerequisite for having sex. Economic conditions and State benefits improved for single mothers, with the availability of social security and, by the 1970s, social housing as well. The sexual freedom championed by the Flower Power generation of the 1960s carried through into the 1970s, when the stigma of having a child outside marriage was beginning to disappear.

* * *

By the 1980s, the nature of adoption had changed once more, no longer seen as a solution to illegitimacy and infertility but as a way to help rebuild the lives of children affected by disability or illness, physical or sexual abuse or neglect, who were in the care system.

The idea that children in care could be adopted had begun to gather pace in the 1970s, influenced by practitioners in the States who had started to recruit families for children previously considered difficult or impossible to adopt. Kay Donley, a charismatic social worker from an American agency that had originated the idea, came to speak in Britain and created a spark of interest amongst social workers. Another influential British practitioner, Jane Rowe, looked at children who were living in foster care and discovered there was nothing planned for those children in the long-term – many spent their lives drifting from one foster placement to another with little prospect of a permanent home. The idea that adoption might be an option for children with disabilities, special needs or from black and minority ethnic groups was already being explored. The notion that this could be extended to other children in the care system began to gain momentum.

In the mid-1970s, and in response to a growing lobby for reform, new legislation introduced a number of important changes. One of the most significant was the introduction of a 'Freeing Order' – a legal Order made by the court dispensing with parental consent to adoption if it was considered in the best interests of the child. By the early 1980s, when the new laws came into practice, there was a big push by local authorities (now required under the new laws to provide a comprehensive adoption service) and voluntary adoption agencies to make adoption placements for children in care.

'Women had more choices, babies weren't available and people who wanted to adopt were looking more broadly,' says Jeanne Kaniuk, OBE, managing director of Coram's Adoption Services, who has worked in the field for 45 years. 'Potential adopters were opening their minds and we were motivated to think about the children's needs.'

Kaniuk remembers when she first became a social worker, before legislation allowed children to be placed for adoption without parental consent.

'I had a caseload of school-age children who came from really sad backgrounds, who were never going to be able to go home safely, whose parents would visit sporadically. Some of them were in lovely foster homes and would remain there for most of their childhood.

But the foster carers had no [legal] rights. We all knew that for most of these children, seeing their parents on a sporadic basis kept unsettling them. Through no fault of their own, these parents would make all sorts of promises they couldn't keep and the children would be terribly disappointed and upset. It was common knowledge among social workers that these poor children weren't actually able to get on with their lives,' she tells me.

'So we were thrilled when the legislation changed, and began to make all kinds of different plans for these children.'

According to Kaniuk, there have been 'huge shifts' in the nature of the children who were being referred for adoption since then. 'We used to place a lot of children with medical conditions such as spina bifida, but with medical advances that doesn't happen very often,' she explains. 'Then came a whole wave of awareness of sexual abuse, and we'd have to think about how to place children who were in care as a result of that.

'Then we became aware of how many young children were at risk and coming into care from backgrounds where either their parents were suffering from mental illness, or substance abuse, the number of babies born drug-addicted because of intrauterine exposure to drugs and so on.'

Adoption was no longer a case of finding a child for a family, or a family for a child – but matching a child's needs to parents' abilities to deal with them. At the same time the culture of secrecy, which had dominated adoption for so many years, was beginning to erode. From the early 1970s, practitioners were being advised on how to help adoptive parents tell their children they were adopted, and promoting the idea that the discussion should be an ongoing one rather than a one-off admission. Evidence was also beginning to emerge about the negative impact secrecy and withholding information could have on an adopted person's sense of self-worth and identity.

One of the most significant pieces of new legislation introduced in the 1976 Adoption Act gave adopted people access to their birth records for the first time, introducing the possibility of tracing birth relatives. But it wasn't without controversy – there was concern in Parliament and some sections of the press that it would open up a Pandora's box. There were fears around the fact that birth mothers could now be traced and contacted and that potential adopters would be deterred because adoption was no longer a clean break from the past. A proviso was put in place to address these anxieties: adopted people were required to attend counselling before they were given any access to information. A watershed in adoption history had been reached, as the culture of secrecy was replaced by a new era of openness.

* * *

In the 1990s, adoption hit a trough and the pendulum swung against it. By 1980 the total number of registered adoptions in Britain had halved to 10,600. That figure halved again to just over 4,000 in 1998 – where it's been around ever since. The decline was mainly down to public policy. In 1989, the Children Act put at its heart the welfare of the child and the importance for local authorities to work in partnership with parents, rather than against them. With some ambivalence still around the issue of children being removed and placed for adoption without consent from the birth parents, resources were channelled into supporting families in difficulty, rather than to adoption services.

'It was the general principle that the responsibility of the state was to maintain a child's relationship with their parents and birth family wherever possible,' explains John Simmonds, director of policy, research and development at CoramBAAF. 'And there was some reluctance to identify adoption as being a potential route out.'

Under the new legislation courts were advised to look at every possible alternative before making a care order. 'So if you're freeing a child for adoption, it has to be the strongest of arguments about why you're doing that, as opposed to not doing that,' says Simmonds, who used to work at BAAF (the British Association for Adoption and Fostering) until 2015, when many of its key services were amalgamated into the Coram group of charities to become CoramBAAF.

Enthusiasm for adoption as an alternative to help children in care, in need of a secure, stable and permanent home, had waned, and wasn't back in favour again with practitioners or policy makers until Tony Blair's Labour Government of 1997 tackled the issue with renewed gusto, announcing in 2000 that he would lead a thorough review of adoption policy, invest money in adoption services, aim to increase the number of looked-after children adopted and overhaul and modernise the legal framework of adoption, among other pledges.

* * *

Almost a century on from its first legislation, adoption remains an ever-evolving, controversial concept, governed by social attitudes, economic conditions and moral and ethical viewpoints that continually shift and divide opinion. What I've always seen as an essentially emotional issue is, in fact, highly political.

Chapter Four

When he was eight years old Gabriel went into hospital to have a small operation on his hand. I hovered over him anxiously as he lay on the bed in his little gown while the anaesthetist held a mask over his face and the nurse held down his legs in case he kicked out. Fear crossed his face before his eyes rolled back and closed shut. I started to cry, and then I couldn't stop. The emotion felt both primal and spontaneous: there's nothing like seeing your child vulnerable to make you understand how deeply you love them.

There have been many moments when this has been brought into sharp relief: from sitting with him in A&E as a doctor clumsily tried to stitch up a gash in his arm to watching him, nervously, in the playground as he tries to infiltrate a game. It doesn't always have to be at vulnerable moments: just watching his little pipe-cleaner legs pump furiously on his bike pedals, or hearing him quietly hum the theme tune to *Wallace and Gromit*, and I can feel the same rush of love.

There are two fundamental questions that lie at the heart of adoption – can you love somebody else's child? And can they love you? With the benefit of hindsight, I know you can. Gabriel is unequivocally my child and I'm confident that, for now, Harry and I are at the centre of his world. But there's no way of knowing this when you adopt. All you can do is hope: it's a leap of faith that co-exists with fear.

Six months had passed since we'd put our adoption plans on hold, but at the beginning of a new year in 2001 we decided we were ready to press on. The prospect of doing nothing, of not venturing down the path to parenthood, didn't feel like an option. We signed up with the adoption agency and Satwinder Sandhu became our social worker. At first I was worried about his age – he was so young, what did he know about life? But his professionalism and gentle manners soon won my confidence. Over the next eight months he learnt more about us than our closest friends, as he raked over the most intimate details of our lives and relationship. The foundation of the homestudy is a Form F1, an extensive questionnaire that covers all areas from your upbringing to your previous relationships, your lifestyle and financial means of support, your understanding and knowledge of children and capacity to be parents. We also had to write our own life stories. Harry was concerned I'd been too honest and laid myself bare but, 'Hey,' I told him, 'that's just the kinda gal I am.'

Every few weeks Satwinder would come to our house and talk to us together for a couple of hours. He'd ask us about our parents' relationship and our school days; our family secrets and religious influences; our sex life and our disagreements; what made us stressed, sad or depressed; our vulnerabilities and strengths; our infertility, and whether we were actively prepared to prevent a pregnancy by using contraception as proof of our commitment to adoption. It felt as if our human rights were being slightly infringed but it also seemed irrelevant: we were going through adoption for the very reason that we couldn't get pregnant, so what was the point in trying to actively prevent it? We hadn't used contraception in years.

The second part of the assessment focused on children – our experiences of them and our expectations for our own child. We were questioned on how we displayed affection to children and our thoughts on the importance of routine, especially at bedtime; our attitudes towards education and nutrition, and whether we expected boys and girls to behave differently; how we'd manage financially and whether we'd have childcare. Then there were the specifics of adoption: how would we cope with the harsh realities of many of the children's backgrounds, and the impact that could have on family life?

At the same time Satwinder conducted interviews with our referees – Sunita, who had known me since we were both 12, and her husband Chris, and our other friends, Ruth and Tim, parents to Louis, who we'd borrowed so extensively. Both Ruth and Sunita are of mixed Asian-British heritage, so could also testify to our ability to embrace other cultures – or at least to the fact we didn't mix in strictly white circles.

Over the months I grew to enjoy our sessions with

Satwinder. I didn't mind talking about myself (I'd been in therapy, after all) or find the process intrusive. There were no skeletons in my cupboard; I felt proud of my life and the people I shared it with. I knew we were being asked to jump through hoops, but at the same time I could understand why. I've read accounts of other adoptive parents who have found the homestudy deeply unsettling with its potential exposure of weakness, threat of being found lacking and the possibility of failure, but I had no such qualms. Of course, no one who has a child naturally is put through the same rigorous process. Biological parents aren't made to assess whether or not they're going to be any good at it, or what their expectations, or motives, might be. Their lives aren't examined or their attitudes judged. Many go into parenthood blithely, if not blindly: to think about it too much could be a deterrent. But in adoption, the child's needs always come first and we had to prove we were capable of meeting them.

All the same, it was a fine balancing act between being honest without disqualifying ourselves: we wanted to pass the test but not sign up for anything we couldn't handle. We had strict parameters and tried to stick to them: we wouldn't consider a child over the age of two, or a sibling group, and held out for a child who could be happy, secure and emotionally attached to us. Looking back on Satwinder's final report now, I can see the efforts we made to be open-minded and diplomatic – we would consider a child with behavioural problems 'but not one that was continually violent, aggressive or destructive'; we would deal with some impairments but not complex physical or educational needs. But it still felt so abstract –

until we had an actual child to consider, we didn't know how we'd feel.

Reading this back now it all sounds cold-hearted, ticking off what we might or might not consider. But we were determined to do right not only by ourselves, but, more importantly, by the children we would be asked to consider. We felt it was essential that we knew our limitations and what we could cope with. We couldn't mess up, or cause these children unnecessary trauma by failing to meet their needs – they'd had enough people do that to them already.

While much of our focus had been on the specifics of adoption, the subtler, but no less fundamental truths had been sidelined. This I discovered at yet more preparation workshops, run by our adoption agency, which left me at times with an overwhelming sadness. We were told about the emotional trauma of adoption and how all parties were brought together through separation and loss.

We learnt about attachment and bonding: how if a baby's basic needs aren't met, particularly in the first six months of life, they will struggle with feelings of love, trust and forming solid relationships as they grow up. We were also given an extract to read from *The Primal Wound*, a book by Nancy Verrier about the adoption experience, which claims that the separation of a child from its birth mother inflicts a wound that never heals. 'The connection between biological mother and child is primal, mystical, mysterious, and everlasting,' writes the author. 'So deep runs the connection between a child and its mother that the severing of the bond results in a profound wound for both, a wound from which neither fully recovers. In the case of adoption, the wound cannot be avoided, but it can and must be acknowledged and understood.'

I've never read the rest of the book – this one extract was enough to put me off. It made me feel helpless and redundant: no matter what we might offer as adoptive parents in terms of support, encouragement and love, it would never be enough. The wound would never heal.

Over the months my conviction waxed and waned until, a few months into our homestudy, Satwinder remarked that he was slightly concerned by our lack of enthusiasm. I leapt to my own defence, launching into a tirade about how I couldn't get excited about something that was still so unknown, that if we were presented with the right child then we would be, and besides, it was hard to be enthusiastic when there were so many negative stories and we were constantly reminded of the difficulty of it all. How could we show enthusiasm over whether or not we could take on a child that had been sexually abused? Or had severe behavioural problems? If he wanted me to dance on the table with joy, I told him, he'd be disappointed. I then burst into tears. Maybe it had been a tactic to get a response. Maybe Satwinder had wanted to see some emotion, but the session left me drained.

'I veer from anger to misery today,' I emailed my friend Jo, the following day. 'What's the way forward? Are we doing the wrong thing? Should we just forget all about it? Or is the perfect child for us out there?' Harry felt the same – we always sang from the same song sheet, whether it was the big or small things in life, and we always tried to have a contingency plan up our sleeve.

I met up with Satwinder recently and we talked about

this moment: his understanding of it was quite different to mine. It wasn't our lack of enthusiasm he was questioning, but rather he felt protective of our interests. He had never worked with a couple, he said, who had been quite so clear about their expectations and what they were prepared to take on board. We weren't prepared to compromise, whereas most other couples showed a little more flexibility. He had no doubts about our capability to be parents, he just wanted to make sure, for our sakes, that it was something we ourselves wanted to do.

A few weeks later we ran off to New York to celebrate my birthday over a long weekend. We stayed with my sister, who was working there, at her apartment in Greenwich Village, and spent the days eating Eggs Benedict for breakfast, shopping in Soho and sipping Cosmopolitans. We strolled through Central Park on a bright, crisp day with blue skies and orange leaves and drank champagne in Grand Central Station. It felt glamorous, carefree and life affirming, and far removed from what we were going through at home. The day before we were due to fly back, a plane en route to Puerto Rico crashed in Queens and all flights were suspended. This was two months after 9/11 and the world was still on red alert. Our trip was extended by a day and so we visited Ground Zero, acrid smoke still rising from the skeletal ruins and photographs of the missing covering its perimeter, which was dotted with prayer stations. The atmosphere was oppressive but for a sobering moment it put our problems into perspective.

For the most part my personal life didn't impinge too greatly on my professional life, although there were times when the two overlapped. Soon after I got back from

New York I had to go to Manchester to interview actor and comedian John Thomson and his wife. It had only recently been revealed in the tabloid press that he was adopted, and that his birth mother, without his knowledge or blessing, had been tracked down. It was a sensitive subject that made him tearful when I brought it up – so much so that he left the room mid-interview. Alone with his wife, I also started to cry. 'I'm so sorry,' I sniffed, 'but I think it's just awful, what's happened,' and I explained about my own adoption plans. It wasn't my finest moment, professionally, but we managed to finish the interview and I haven't cried in one since.

By the end of the year, and the homestudy, I felt much happier. Not excited as such, but something bordering on anticipation. A date had been set in the New Year for us to go to panel – the group of adoption specialists and professionals who decide from the information presented to them (including the homestudy) whether or not you can adopt – and I began to allow myself thoughts such as 'This time next year…' Of course, we had no idea when we were going to become a family – unlike a pregnancy, which has a start and finishing date – but we weren't prepared for the long wait that was to follow.

We weren't surprised when we were accepted – I would have been shocked if we hadn't – so there was no whooping it up or popping of champagne corks. Instead we had a quiet drink down the local pub. But at least now we could start considering potential children, and possibly be matched with them.

A few weeks later, my friend Susan gave birth to her first baby, a boy called Jack, and asked me to be godmother. A week after his arrival I went to visit and watched as she gently rubbed olive oil into his prune-like skin, looking like a woman in love. How would I ever be able to love another's child like that? I didn't know what felt worse, my sense of loss or envy of her happiness. These aren't easy or pretty emotions to admit to, especially as I was trying to balance them with genuine happiness for my friend, but for the next few days I fell into a deep pit of self-pity, and my envy of other people who had children was exhausting.

My perspective on life became skewed. I never got what I wanted; life didn't treat me kindly; nothing was ever easy. It gnawed away at my confidence and self-esteem, and I felt unworthy of happiness – especially from something so seemingly simple, universal and fundamental as being able to conceive and give birth. 'Everyone has children,' I wrote bitterly in my diary, 'except us.'

Our coping mechanism had always been to plan full, busy lives. I needed to have something to look forward to, so we went on a lot of holidays. In two years we visited Rome and New York, practiced yoga in Spain and Sri Lanka and spent a month in India, shortly before we went to the approval panel. These trips gave me a focus, reminding me that life was exciting, that the world had wide horizons and was rich in possibilities. We weren't stuck in London, hopeless and childless. Of course, we were privileged to go on these trips: we had the means to escape. But, while it was hugely therapeutic to run away, our sense of emptiness was still there when we came back.

A few months after we'd been passed by the approval panel we put in an offer for a small, cheap and ancient apartment in Southern Spain and began the protracted negotiations to buy it. But the sense of rattling around, waiting for something to happen, persisted. 'Our friends' lives are given meaning by their children,' said Harry. 'We have to dig a lot deeper to find ours.' Despite the path to adoption being seemingly littered with obstacles and false hopes, this was another reason why we continued to navigate it: it gave us a sense of purpose and meaning, something to fight for.

At times we may have been angry with the world but we were never angry with each other; we were united in our cause, which only made us closer. We had made a commitment to adoption, and rarely disagreed.

That would come later.

* * *

A popular story that pops up in certain sections of the press is the 'Too Posh To Adopt' one. It usually focuses on a white, middle-class couple who, despite their best efforts and intentions, fail to adopt a child in Britain due to intrusive questioning, bureaucratic red tape, the incompetency of social services and the discouragement of interracial adoption. Over the next few years we witnessed, and experienced, all of those things. My friend Vicky, who went through the adoption process a year before us, was turned down by one child's set of social workers because they didn't have curtains in the front room and had builders working on the house. She was also criticised for not being prepared to give up work permanently and advised to turn her study into a nursery to 'show willing'. Maybe it's only now, from the perspective of a stable family life, that I can be more understanding of the process and why it can feel like there are too many ridiculous obstacles to overcome – when all you want to do is give a child a home. But we frequently felt beaten by a system that seemed stacked against us. This was largely because our feelings and needs weren't a priority – those of the child had to come first. Although that's exactly how it should be, it didn't always seem fair. Often we felt as if we'd been found lacking, or that we couldn't quite prove our worth, or that our feelings were of no significance at all.

Soon after we were approved, Satwinder began to send us Form Es, which carried details of children up for adoption. There was Brandon, a two-year-old boy who was born addicted to heroin. His grandmother had been murdered and his mother, who had never been to school, had disappeared. Brandon was developmentally delayed and his general prognosis was uncertain. There was two-and-a-half-year-old Mark, whose temper was very violent in one so young and who would shield his face with his arm whenever a stranger approached. On one visit a social worker had found him in a cot in an empty room, the floor covered in used hypodermic syringes. Then there was Lewis, whose delayed development was put down to the fact that he was under-stimulated in his first few months, when he'd been strapped in a car seat and left in front of the TV for hours on end. He was over two years old and couldn't talk, rarely cried or drew attention to himself.

I've made up the names here and used amalgams of real cases, but they're pretty representative of some of the forms we read. I'd absorb the details, look at their pictures – they were so beautiful and sweet – and feel I'd been exposed to a cruel, hellish world, the underbelly of life. Sometimes we'd know immediately these children weren't for us. Other times there'd be something that resonated, and drew us back – the description of a gentle temperament, or an easy laugh. We'd try and imagine them in our lives, and almost convince ourselves that we were equipped to deal with their problems. Then, feeling awful, we'd turn them down. The sense of guilt at rejecting these children and not offering them a home never quite left us.

The 'pick and choose' process felt callous, especially when we'd read *Children Who Wait*, a catalogue-style publication issued by the charity Adoption UK, which featured children who were looking for a family. The children would be wearing their Sunday best and their biggest smiles in the photographs, which were accompanied by brief, upbeat descriptions. Harry and I would try and look for clues – what do 'needs constant stimulation', 'requires firm boundaries' or 'making good progress' actually mean? Were potential problems glossed over in the same way as an estate agent's patter?

I once heard a radio interview with Barbara Harris, the American founder of the US charity Project Prevention, which offers women who have a drug addiction a choice of sterilisation or long-term implant contraception, which is reversible, and for which they are paid. Her belief, quite simply, is that addicts should not have children. In her opinion, babies born to addicts are in withdrawal, often underweight, with serious medical problems and, if they survive, are destined to a bleak future. Meanwhile, their mothers continue to have children. What about the moral implications of paying vulnerable women to be sterilised? What happens to those women who come off drugs and want to start a family, but have been sterilised? What right does anyone have to tell a woman she can't have children? To any criticism that was levelled at her, her answer was the same: 'I don't care.' Her beliefs were resolute and steadfast. It was shocking but impressive. And at times during the interview, to my horror, I felt a stirring of sympathy for what she was saying. I'd read too many Form Es for her opinions not to make some sort of skewed sense. And then I felt ashamed of myself for agreeing.

If matters weren't complicated enough, it felt as if we were caught up in what appeared to be a chaotic, incompetent and discourteous system. Requests for children's details would go ignored. Phone calls weren't returned, or we wouldn't hear back for weeks. We never got as far as meeting the social worker for any child we were interested in. When we did eventually secure our first meeting, it was farcical. We were visited by a bored-looking social worker for a toddler called Kaly (not her real name), who might have had attention deficit hyperactivity disorder (ADHD), she wasn't sure, or she may also have had mild cerebral palsy. 'But it's not as if she's gaga or anything,' she said, sticking her tongue out of the side of her mouth. We sat in stunned silence. I asked about the little girl's relationship with her mother. 'Oh, you don't have to worry about that,' said the social worker with a wave of her hand. 'The mother doesn't even want to see her.' We were asked a couple of questions about multi-racial awareness and childcare, and then off she went to interview some other couples. She left knowing nothing about us, on which she would later base her decision: she had done Kaly even more of a disservice.

Several days later we found out about a family we knew whose adoption of a four-year-old boy had broken down. The mum was a friend of a friend and I'd met her several times before, to pick her brains and ask advice. I'd been reassured by their apparent happiness – their little boy seemed well balanced and bonded to them; she in turn seemed calm and confident. But after a year, she'd suffered some sort of breakdown and felt she could no longer cope. The boy was taken away and put back in care, waiting to be placed with another family.

I was shocked, and couldn't believe that the family I'd found so encouraging and positive had so irrevocably fallen apart. That night, unable to sit in our flat but wanting to talk, Harry and I walked endlessly around our local streets, trying to understand what had happened. The details were sketchy but I immediately identified with the mum. Her experience had tapped into my deepest fears. What if that happened to me? What if I couldn't cope and had to send a child back? What if my failure ruined everybody's lives? Adoption became a terrifying prospect.

The fear carried on for a few weeks, until I called our social worker Satwinder for an emergency chat. He listened calmly. So would he adopt? I challenged him. Yes, he said, he would, adding that we had to focus on the positive; that many of these children came with labels attached to them, and you had to try and look beyond that.

He then told us (to my huge relief) that another family had been chosen for Kaly, but that the social workers for Aidan, a ten-month-old baby boy, wanted to set up a meeting. We'd been sent his details but in the midst of my crisis we'd dismissed them. Now we felt open to persuasion again.

Aidan's mother had taken cocaine during her pregnancy but Aidan was meeting all his milestones. Armed with a packet of chocolate biscuits and an immaculately tidy and hoovered flat, we put on our best performance. We were grilled for two hours, all the while having no idea that they were considering other couples at the same time. A few days later, we were turned down – for not being Irish or Catholic, which, apparently, we'd need to be to reflect Aidan's cultural background. This had happened to us before. When we'd once made enquiries about an 18-month-old girl, Megan, who had been featured in *Children Who Wait*, we were told we didn't reflect her cultural heritage: she had a black grandfather. In addition, the couple chosen for Aidan lived outside London – which was considered another bonus – and the woman was giving up work to be a stay-at-home mum.

It was hard not to feel angry. We were clearly never going to be Irish or Catholic enough, so why had our expectations been falsely raised? 'They shouldn't have seen us,' I wrote angrily in my diary. 'They are so obsessed with prioritising the child, they forget they're dealing with vulnerable human beings.'

Not all social workers we came across were incompetent or insensitive. We met many who were helpful, kind and, remarkably, able to meet everyone's needs. Satwinder, at whom I directed most of my frustration, was (and still is) one of them: we let off steam and he listened. It had been three-and-a-half years since we'd had our first ever meeting about adoption, and a year-and-a-half since we'd been approved, and we were no closer to being a family. I was tempted, I said, to try other adoption agencies. He suggested we might have problems finding one to take us on. We had very strict parameters on the children we were willing to consider and we weren't spring chickens either. But I thought I'd give it a bash, and so I spent an afternoon making a series of desperate phone calls to various local authority adoption agencies. One told me they were no longer recruiting white couples who wanted healthy, pre-school age children. Another suggested we make a promotional flyer about ourselves and our strong points and send it in. Yet another listened very sympathetically but explained their books were full. It was hopeless. Suitably chastened, we returned to Satwinder. At least he was on our side.

Meanwhile, we'd begun to make alternative plans. The more time passed, the more the possibility of adoption seemed to recede. We couldn't let go of the idea completely, but just for our own sense of self-worth, and sanity, we needed to remind ourselves that there was a future to be had without children. At the beginning of the year we'd finally completed on the flat in Spain, which we'd fly out to every six weeks or so. The previous owners had literally stripped it bare – including the kitchen sink and light fittings – so we started from scratch, cleaning, painting and scouring second-hand shops for furniture. Now we lived in a parallel world, completely absorbed in the little town and the home we were creating there. We grew used to the ebb and flow of Spanish life – from the hourly chiming of the church bells to the annual running of bulls down our narrow street every Semana Santa; from queuing for hours in shops while old ladies chatted about the madness of the two-week summer *feria* when the whole town slept all day and partied all night. Too hot to move during the day, we'd go to the beach in the late afternoon, take a long walk at sunset and eat fresh seafood at midnight at one of the many cafés. If Plan A hadn't worked out by the end of the year, we promised ourselves, then we'd put Plan B into action and move to Spain. 'I can't stand the thought of my life being the same this time next year,' I wrote somewhat melodramatically in my diary. 'In fact, it can't be.' My thoughts veered from, 'How can we adopt when we're involved in all this?' to 'How can I possibly imagine a future without children?'

It was Molly who brought everything to a head. In September 2003, we were sent details of a ten-month-old baby girl who had been born with neonatal abstinence syndrome (NAS) – her mother had taken heroin, or crack cocaine, or both, throughout her pregnancy, and Molly was born with an addiction. She had been through withdrawal and although she was slightly fractious and had trouble sleeping, she was reaching her developmental milestones – at least as far as a baby of that age could. Feeling fairly non-committal, we agreed to meet her social workers in October. Two days after meeting them, we were told that they wanted to go ahead with us – which meant we were the only potential adopters in the frame and they wanted to move towards making the match official.

It was the furthest we'd ever gone along the process and I flew into a blind panic: it had all happened too quickly and I was wracked with doubt. I wrote one of my pros and cons lists. My reasons for going ahead, looking back, were all negative: 'I'd have to live with the regret of saying no', 'I'd have to live with the sadness of being childless', 'We've come so far, how can we turn back now?' and even 'It might tear Harry and I apart if we don't'. My reasons against bordered on the hysterical: 'The child will reject me', 'I don't want a daughter – I want a son', 'I'll feel as if I've lost my life and made the biggest mistake ever'. My life felt under siege. That was before I'd even considered how Molly's early experiences could impact on her later life.

Harry, although not quite as tormented, was shocked at the speed with which events seemed to be moving. We knew hardly anything about this little girl and yet we were being chosen as her potential parents. 'It's like getting a mail order bride,' he said. 'Or being proposed to on the first date.'

We were sent a home video and she couldn't have been sweeter. Pretty, smiley and animated, she was doing all the right things, making all the right responses. I was reminded of a story we'd heard in one of our workshops of a woman who'd been desperate to adopt a baby. When finally matched with a perfectly healthy three-month-old, she held the baby in her arms and cried. She couldn't go through with it. Maybe it was fear, or maybe the reality just didn't match up to her fantasy.

The fact that it was my 40th birthday in November made our decision seem all the more significant. I wanted it to be a birthday I'd remember, so we invited our closest friends over to Spain and spent the weekend celebrating. It felt good to be childless. A few weeks later, at the end of

November, I flew to Mauritius for a shoot and interview with a world-number-one male tennis player. We stayed in one of the island's luxury hotels, where I sat by an infinity pool overlooking a turquoise sea, sipping strawberry daiquiris and recovering from jet lag, feeling I could easily get used to the lifestyle. Adoption seemed another world away. For a couple of weeks I managed to switch off.

But back home I was thrown into indecision. Actually, it was more fear, made worse by the fact that Harry was so much calmer than me: his was the voice of reason, mine the voice of panic. Molly haunted me – wherever I went, there she was. I found it hard to concentrate on anything else. She began to feel like a threat: I didn't want my life to change, I wanted it to be the same, just Harry and me, with no one else getting in the way. I feared for our relationship. What if this decision completely polarised us? What if we couldn't reach an agreement? What effect would it have on our marriage if I said I didn't want to go ahead? We'd never disagreed up until now – was this it?

A few days later, unable to work at home, I went to visit Harry, who at the time was working as an aborist near the Tate Modern. We popped along to see The Weather Project, the giant artificial orange sun that lit up the Turbine Hall, and lay underneath it for hours, joining the floor pattern made by the visiting crowds. We talked and talked, and I learnt that his feelings weren't quite so different to mine. We weren't in two separate camps, as I'd feared, his was just a more measured approach: he wasn't scared, but he wasn't excited either. He wasn't ready to give up on her just yet, but he didn't want to press on with something unless we were both sure. He described himself as 'battle weary'.

'Anyway,' he added, 'I can't make a decision without us both being happy about it. And if you're not happy, then neither am I.'

I needed to get to the root of my uncertainty, and why I wasn't prepared to make the same leap of faith that I might have done with another child. We were also still waiting to have certain clarifications about Molly's medical report, but so far the social workers were dragging their heels. It had been almost three months since we'd first been sent details and we were no nearer to making a decision.

I wanted to make an informed decision, not an emotional one, and so I decided to arm myself with knowledge. I spent hours in a specialist library, reading about the long-term effects of opiates and crack cocaine on babies, but drew no conclusions. Many of the studies had been carried out in the States in the 1990s on 'crack babies' who were materially disadvantaged and emotionally neglected, despite any drug abuse. These weren't studies I felt I could trust. I spoke to drug charities, who reassured me many children born to addicted mothers grow up to lead healthy lives. But I still didn't feel reassured.

Christmas came and went and by the New Year, we still hadn't made a decision. The incompetence of Molly's social workers didn't help – they were giving us information on a drip feed, most of which was conflicting. I felt no excitement, joy, commitment or enthusiasm. 'How do you know you won't regret your decision ten years down the line?' asked a friend. I didn't know, but I was trying to weigh up the risks. What would I regret more – saying no to a child, and later questioning the decision? Or saying yes, and living with the consequences?

'I can't get past my fear,' I wrote. 'I'm trying to, but I can't. I've failed.'

We had a meeting with Satwinder, who told us maybe our doubts about Molly could have been overcome but the incompetence of the social services couldn't, and that she'd been hanging around in our lives for too long, when she shouldn't have been. He was as frustrated as we were. There had been months of deliberation, uncertainty and waiting for information. Perhaps if they'd been more efficient, if we'd had more confidence in them, then we may have made a different decision. But I was reassured that, by saying no, we'd made the right one. With that came an immediate sense of relief, but also sadness. In the past few weeks I'd revisited old feelings about not being able to have my own biological child, and had a sudden sense of my own mortality. My sister and I were at the end of the line: who would we pass on our family stories to? Who was going to look through my photo albums? Who would play with the odd toys that Harry and I had been surreptitiously collecting? But it was never going to be Molly.

'I looked into my future,' I wrote in my diary, 'and I couldn't see her.'

Saying no to Molly at the beginning of the year left us feeling as if there was nowhere else to go. If we said no to her, who would we be able to say yes to? Harry and I couldn't bring ourselves to discuss it. Satwinder suggested we went to see a counsellor who specialised in adoption issues, but our first – and only – session wasn't a success. I sat and cried through most of it, while Harry didn't say much. When he did, he said he'd pretty much reached the end of the adoption road and couldn't see us continuing with it any further. But I couldn't bear the thought of giving up.

A decision hovered over us, waiting to land.

* * *

From time to time Gabriel tests out difficult concepts with me in conversation. Once we were chatting about children at school and who was his first, second and third best friend. Ever the child myself, I asked him if I was his first best Mummy. 'No,' he said. 'You're about the third or fourth.' I found comfort in the fact that he didn't have anyone else in mind for the first and second places, but he still came out with a long list of reasons as to why I couldn't be top – I shout in his ear, make him wear uncomfortable pants and don't let him watch TV in the mornings, etc. 'And anyway,' he added, 'how do I know there isn't someone better out there?' He'd got me there. 'You're my best boy,' I told him. 'But there might be a better boy than me,' he replied.

The conversation is rich in possible interpretations. Would a biological mother and child have the same chat? Was he only asking these things because he's adopted? But it also has a certain logic: Gabriel has known other mothers – his birth mother, and his foster carer. He knows, therefore, that it's possible to have more than one mother. But I know that, after everything we had gone through, and all we'd experienced, we'd found the right boy, the *only* boy, who would have done for us.

* * *

Three months after turning Molly down, Satwinder called with details of a boy who was almost two years old. I heard his name and felt an instant sense of recognition. When we were sent his photo – he was wearing pyjamas, his foster mother's furry slippers and a huge grin, his little hands clenched in excitement – the sense of familiarity grew. 'Ah, there you are,' we thought. We began to project our fantasies onto the photograph. It was dangerous and exciting but we couldn't help ourselves. We'd say hello to him every morning.

A meeting with his social workers had been scheduled for the following week and we counted down the days. The night before I couldn't sleep. I don't remember much about the meeting, apart from watching a home video of Gabriel made by his foster carers. He made me laugh. Bright, boisterous and cheeky, he had a beautifully expressive face. He was described to us as spontaneous and outgoing, a 'lovely, adorable little boy,' according to his foster mother, a child who drew attention to himself and was a real pleasure to everyone.

'The boy has spirit,' I wrote in my diary.

It's at this stage, I guess, that I should write something about his background – but I'm not going to. One of the first things we were told when we set off on this journey is that your adopted child's history is theirs alone, and no one else has the right to disclose it. I fully subscribe to that. But like most children who are placed for adoption, Gabriel had a difficult family background from which he had been largely protected. He had been looked after by his foster family since a baby and was meeting all his developmental milestones – that is, he was a perfectly normal, healthy little boy.

Gabriel is of mixed white/African-Caribbean heritage

but his social workers were prepared to consider us, which, at the time was still unusual. Since we lived in a multi-racial area, it was felt that we'd be able to reflect and engage in Gabriel's cultural heritage. In fact, we were the only couple they were considering, which came as a relief. The next day, I was due to fly out to Nairobi on a short work trip. That morning, Satwinder rang me at work to say we'd been chosen for Gabriel. I got off the phone and burst into tears. Three of my colleagues burst into tears as well. Then I rang Harry and he burst into tears too, and came straight to meet me for a drink before I headed off to Heathrow. We sat grinning at each other at the bar.

The next few months felt like being in love – I was preoccupied, distracted, and nothing else apart from Gabriel seemed important. There was also a feeling of fragility and disbelief – that he could be taken away from us at any minute. The final decision wouldn't be made until the matching panel met and made their decision as to whether or not we could adopt Gabriel, which wasn't scheduled for another month, although we felt confident we'd be matched. We passed without a hitch. The delight and relief was mixed with a slight sense of the ridiculous – we had been chosen to be the parents of a child we hadn't even met yet. We were making the biggest commitment of our lives – far greater than the one we'd made to each other when we married – and we had no idea how we'd feel when we met him. What if we didn't like each other?

Shortly afterwards I flew to Pakistan, where for the next ten days I'd be travelling the country with Marie Stopes International to research and write a feature on family planning. It was one of the biggest commissions of my career so far and I felt exhilarated and terrified, not just by the subject, about which I knew nothing, but also at the prospect of visiting a country where relations with the UK were not at their most positive. I interviewed stern imans in Karachi about contraception and majestically beautiful elders in an Afghanistan refugee camp about young girls and marriage. The Pakistani people I met couldn't have been more warm or hospitable but there was no escaping the threatening undercurrent – I chose not to walk the streets on my own. However, I felt strangely invincible: we were adopting Gabriel, so nothing was going to happen to me. I also witnessed firsthand what it was *really* like to struggle with parenthood – many of the women I met in the Marie Stopes clinics had nine or ten children. And I was worrying about coping with one…

Once back home from Pakistan Harry and I indulged in a bit of light relief by making a home video for Gabriel. Filmed by my sister, its purpose was for us to introduce ourselves in a bright, jolly and entertaining way, and for him to become familiar with us. It was a humiliating experience, resulting in two minutes of film, which took us two days to make. I don't think any footage from the first day made the final edit. We were both hungover, having celebrated our wedding anniversary the night before, and I came over more *Tomorrow's World* than *Play School* presenter, all stiff-necked and clipped voice. On day two we fared a little better, having written a script; I even put my hair in bunches. We toured his tiny bedroom, which we'd begun gingerly to decorate, introduced the cats and ran around like idiots in the park across the road.

'I hope he's not traumatised by it,' I said to Harry.

The day before we were due to begin our new life with Gabriel, we threw a party. Our friends had bought us cards and brought gifts for him. We wanted to celebrate our final day as a childless couple. But no matter how much I tried, I couldn't imagine how my world was going to be from now on. Nor could I bring myself to say that I was going to be a mother: I hadn't yet earned that title.

Chapter Five

Every so often we sit down and watch a TV programme or film together. Usually it's more 'fraught' than 'fun' bickering over what to watch, but we can always agree on *Modern Family*, an American sitcom based around an extended family and their respective domestic set-ups. We like it because it's funny, but also because it subverts the idea of the traditional nuclear family, and shows the alternatives.

We were hooked from the first episode, in which Mitchell, who is gay, and his partner Cameron ('Cam') bring home their adopted daughter Lily from Vietnam. They are on the flight back to the US, feeling nervous and self-conscious, when a fellow passenger remarks on Lily and a couple of 'cream puffs'. Mitchell leaps to his feet and delivers an impassioned speech to the plane, defending his family, before realising that the woman is referring to the cream-filled pastries that Lily is eating.

The daft play on words is funny but Harry and I

could also relate to the feelings of embarrassment and heightened sensitivity when in a public place with a newly-acquired adopted child. Even now, Harry cringes at the memory of a bus trip back from a paddling pool in the first week Gabriel lived with us in which he cried and screamed the whole journey. 'It felt like everyone was looking at us, thinking, "Who are those two people with that child?"' he says.

We are a straight, white middle-class couple in a long-term marriage so in terms of convention, we pretty much tick all the boxes. But that sense of scrutiny, of being under examination and possibly judged must be felt more keenly by those in the minority who don't conform to the traditional nuclear family – if you are a lesbian, gay or single adoptive parent.

'I'm very conscious of it,' says Fliss, a social worker who has two adopted sons with her wife Karin. In fact, she enjoys challenging some of the assumptions about same-sex couples. 'If I'm in a shop with the boys and say something like, "Let's get this for Mummy," I assume I'm going to be mistaken for the childminder. So I go out of my way sometimes if I know somebody's listening and will say things like, "Give that to Mama," so they know there are two mums.'

Discrimination on the grounds of sexual orientation across adoption or fostering is illegal, and single people have been able to adopt since legislation was first introduced in 1926. Over the past few decades family make up has changed – birth families come in all different shapes, sizes and colours, society has become more tolerant and adoption practice has had to reflect those changes. In the year up to end of March 2014, seven per cent of children were adopted in England by same-sex couples (either in a civil partnership or not), which was up by one per cent from the previous year (according to figures from BAAF taken from government reports).

Even so, prejudice still exists. While I've been writing this chapter, Northern Ireland's health minister, Jim Wells, resigned after allegedly making homophobic remarks on the 2015 General Election campaign trail, causing furore when he said in one debate that child abuse was more rife amongst gay couples. The row was compounded by a doorstep exchange in which Wells allegedly told a lesbian couple with children that he didn't agree with their lifestyle.

Fashion designers Domenico Dolce and Stefano Gabbana sent shockwaves through celebrity circles in particular when, in 2015, they denounced gay adoption, 'chemical offsprings' and 'synthetic children' born into same-sex families through IVF and despite being gay themselves, announced, 'the only family is a traditional one.' Sir Elton John, father of two sons from a surrogate mother with his husband, David Furnish, was furious and called for a boycott of their label.

Around the same time, a new book, *Modern Families: Parents and Children in New Family Forms* by child psychologist Susan Golombok, asserted that gay parents not only bring up children as well as straight ones, but that statistically they may be better parents. She divides her book into three categories: 'traditional', which is heterosexual married couples; 'non-traditional' families, headed by single parents, cohabiting parents or step-parents; and 'new' families, which include lesbian-mother families, gay-father families and families created by IVF and surrogacy. 'When there are differences between new families and traditional families,' said Golombok in *The Sunday Times*, 'studies show it's the new families that show more involved, committed, positive parenting.' She added: 'When you think about it, the parents of these families are people who have often gone through infertility or faced a lot of social disapproval, or sometimes both. So only people that really, really want to be parents stay the course. It's often so difficult that if you weren't committed, you'd just drop off along the way.'

Although Golombok is not talking specifically about adoptive parents here, either lesbian, gay or single, the same applies. The driving force behind any adoption is the desire to be parents, whatever our relationship status or sexual orientation. But ultimately it's not about our rights: it's about the rights of children who need a loving, caring home in which to grow and thrive. For this chapter, I wanted to explore these non-traditional family set-ups, to find out if the road to adoption had been any tougher than ours, and any differences in parenting experience.

As a gay, single man, Gordon, 40, is a rarity in the adoption world. 'I think I know all the others,' he says in a joke about his community. He's also a bit of a character. Born and raised in Oklahoma, he moved to the UK in 2005 after working in New York for several years, first as a pre-school assistant and then a social worker. He adopted his son William, six, whom he talks about with great love and pride, 18 months ago, through the adoption agency PACT.

'I don't like to be sentimental but he's like a revelation,' he says of his son. 'He's bright, curious, funny, loving and easy to get along with.'

I was introduced to Gordon by our social worker Satwinder, who championed his ambition to become a father, despite what appeared to be some serious obstacles. Gordon, who is small and neat, with a knowing sense of humour, easy laugh and youthful appearance, first thought about adopting when he came out as gay at 15.

'One of the first things my mother said was, "I'll never be a grandmother,"' he says with a rueful smile. 'I had thought about being a father, even though I was very young, but when she said that I thought, "Well, I'll adopt a child."'

It was while working in a parenting and family centre in Greenwich Village in the late 1990s that the idea to become a parent took hold.

'I was really playful and fun with the kids. We'd take them on adventures around the city, to the zoo and the park, and I could really connect with them. In downtown New York it wasn't unusual to have a gay male nanny, or playschool teacher – in fact, it was a cool thing for young, middle-class couples. They kept telling me I'd make a great dad.'

He'd talk about adopting with his friends but it wasn't until he retrained as a social worker, specialising in child protection work, and moved to London in 2005 that the possibility became more of a reality. It was the year before 'gay weddings' became law with the Civil Partnership Act and, from 2006, unmarried couples, including same-sex couples, were able to adopt jointly. Up until then, only one person in a couple could become the legal adopter. The social climate was changing and Gordon's confidence was growing.

'The thing about being an adopter and doing it by yourself is that you must be able to imagine yourself being a parent. OK, everyone has to do that, but as a gay, single person, you have to be able to give yourself permission, especially when the law of the land in any way seems unwelcome.'

He made some initial enquiries, but felt he wasn't yet ready to take on any parental commitments as he was still, as he describes it, 'Chaotic in my personal adventures.' During his spell in New York he had taken recreational drugs, which had, at times, impacted on his mental health, resulting in treatment and medication. He knew he'd have to 'figure things out' if he wanted to become a parent, which he did over the next six years, by going into therapy. By 2007 he'd stopped drinking and taking drugs.

In 2011, he made his first initial enquiry with PACT adoption agency, knowing that, 'things about me would be called into question.' Throughout an initial, two-hour interview, Gordon didn't reveal his drug history: 'I knew it would be found out eventually but the question in the initial interview was something like, "Do you have any medical conditions that would impact..." and I could truthfully answer that I didn't. It felt like another life by that time and I didn't want to risk being discounted before I had the chance to explain it in my own way during the assessment.'

However, his medical records revealed not only his drug history but also subsequent battles with mental health. Feeling that her professional relationship with Gordon had been compromised, his social worker withdrew from his case and his application was put on hold while a full assessment was carried out. Additional social and professional references were sought, as was a second medical opinion from a psychiatrist.

'Had he been completely honest in his initial interview all this would have been potentially cleared up before we formally started,' says Satwinder, who at the time was the director of adoption and fostering at PACT and carried out the assessment. 'But I thought Gordon was well motivated to be a parent. He had given it a lot of thought and I felt his ability to be reflective could be a useful skill when dealing with an adopted child. I could sense his desire and passion to parent and wish to take his life in that direction, which is always key.'

Gordon's application was allowed to continue and his homestudy proved relatively straightforward. His support network was scrutinised – 'I had to prove there were a lot of people in the vicinity who would help me' – but his sexual orientation or lifestyle wasn't.

'There was none of that, and I think those close to me, even the social worker, would know that I would have flipped at the suggestion of sexual impropriety,' he says. 'Although I know someone it did happen to. The social worker came round and said, "Why do you want to do this? You're a single gay man, running around, partying." He said, "That is offensive – you are putting all sorts of cultural assumptions on me which have nothing to do with me."'

When it came to the sort of children he'd consider, his parameters were broad. Having worked with abused and traumatised children who, he says, 'I'd loved, and would have taken home,' he knew what was, 'on the cards.'

A few months after he'd been approved, Gordon was sent a profile of William, who had been removed from his birth family after witnessing severe domestic violence perpetrated by one of his parents. 'Everybody had said, "No" to him, and I thought, "I'm not going to."'

'In early foster care he grunted like an animal, scratched himself bloody at night and everyone thought he was unadoptable because of his past. There was a lot of deterministic thinking around him. Also, no one described him as smart, which really irritated me because he clearly is. He wasn't a difficult child.'

William came to live with Gordon in the summer of 2013, when he was four-and-a-half, and settled in more or less immediately.

At the end of his first year at school he told Gordon that his friends had asked why he didn't have a mummy.

'I said to him, "So what did you tell them?" and he said, "I told them that when I came there just wasn't one."'

Gordon says he doesn't feel, 'judged or discriminated against' for being a single, gay parent, although he suspects he makes the fathers at school uncomfortable with the realisation that, 'no matter how hands-on they are, they're not as hands-on as me.'

What he has struggled with, he admits, is the loneliness, especially in the first six months. 'The thing that caved in on me which I didn't expect was, "This is all up to you. It doesn't matter what your mum says or your friends, they don't make the final decisions."'

'There were times when I wanted to be alone as I knew

I had to get used to it,' he adds. 'I would sit in a chair and think, "In 12 hours' time he's going to be up again!"' But mostly it was fine and he thrived on the one-to-one attention. If he was to advise other single male adopters it would be to, 'give yourself permission to be a father. You have to be able to spend an enormous amount of time with your child and be prepared for the loneliness, that quivering at night. But I would say that to any single parent.'

Any regrets? 'No, I can barely imagine my life before,' he says. 'It was meant to be. He is my child in every way.'

Giving himself permission to be a parent is something Ian, a hairdresser in central London, has struggled with. Almost five years ago he adopted his son Nathan with his long-term partner Andrew when Nathan was seven-and-a-half and, despite a difficult beginning, they have settled down into a stable, loving family.

Ian, a gentle-mannered and handsome 55-year-old, is honest about how he has struggled, at times, with his identity as a gay man.

'I had thought about having kids, but being gay, I just never thought it would happen. Back in the early 1980s, when there was the whole health scare about AIDS, you almost didn't want to say you were a gay man,' he says. 'Also, growing up in the 1970s there weren't any good role models – you had people like Larry Grayson, so not the most positive image!'

His fear was that, as two men, he and Andrew would be 'inadequate' as parents. 'My idea was always that a child should have a mum and a dad, and could never be happy with two dads. Maybe with two mums, because of the whole maternal thing… I've always worried about what people think, for right or wrong reasons.'

A happy afternoon spent with a friend and their children became the catalyst to change his mind: 'I got in the car and felt really upset; I wanted to cry. I really felt not having children was something I had missed out on, but that I was too old.'

As soon as he began making enquiries, however, Ian felt encouraged. It was post-2005, when same-sex couples could adopt, and he found a sympathetic, supportive independent agency with whom, he says, they've had a 'lovely' experience.

The fact that they were two men worked to their advantage with Nathan, who was taken into care at the age of five, having been mainly raised by his half-brother after being abandoned by his mother as a baby. 'They [the adoption agency] thought he would struggle if he went to a single woman because he'd always been brought up by a man,' says Ian. 'He's very loving – and I would have found it hard if he hadn't been. As soon as he met us he gave us a big hug and a kiss and he's always been like that.'

Nathan is more sensitive about his birth family than he is about living with two men. 'Someone said to him once, "Your mum didn't love you" and that really upset him, but we haven't had many issues about him having two dads.

'He did once have a friend who was going to come round for a sleepover, but Nathan said to us, "Actually, Daddy, his father doesn't like gay men." I said, "Not everyone does" and it wasn't a big issue.

'About two years after we adopted him, he said, "Can I tell you something? You're not going to like it, but my initial wish was to have a mum and dad, but I'm really happy now." He really thought he was going to upset us, but it was very sweet that he felt he could tell us, after all that time.'

Despite some challenging behaviour – his temper tantrums were so severe that Ian would have to hold him so he wouldn't harm himself – Nathan has thrived.

'It feels so much easier now,' says Ian. 'It probably took around three years, but we're definitely a family. And I still think it's the most rewarding thing I've ever done.'

He no longer feels that Nathan has missed out in not having a mum and dad. 'Most people say to me, "Look, you're doing a fantastic job. He's lucky to have you," which is a lovely thing to say and helps to reassure me.'

* * *

'There are so many different ways to have a family these days – it's like Heinz 57,' says Fliss, 39, who has been in a relationship with Karin for 19 years. 'Civil partnership has helped enormously, and that same-sex couples are seen as a family unit themselves, whether with or without children.'

Going through the assessment process to adopt their two boys, now aged four and three-and-a-half, 18 months ago, they weren't so much discriminated against as pigeonholed.

'There were certain elements that our social worker made assumptions about. She asked about our lifestyle at one point, and seemed hooked on the idea that gays and lesbians went out every night, and bed-hopped. She asked how we'd cope with not partying at the weekend, and we sort of went "Sorry?"' she laughs. 'Generally speaking, we're not that kind of people.'

Prepared to consider a sibling group up to the age of four, the only restriction they made was in terms of gender. 'We didn't want two girls. Four women in the same house... we felt we needed a bit of testosterone! And that was based on our sexuality in terms of being two women.'

It was only when their eldest son started nursery that he began to ask, 'Why don't we have a daddy? Where's our daddy?' 'We just said, "Well, some families have two mummies, some families have two daddies, some families have a mummy and a daddy, and some families have only one." We dealt with it that way,' says Fliss, who along with Karin also joined a local gay parenting group to extend their social circle. Both their fathers, and their best male friend, are on hand to play positive male role models – something they were asked to prove they could provide during their assessment.

'When the boys' foster carer found out we were two women, I think she was worried. I don't think she's homophobic in any way, but they're a traditional family. It's been an eye-opener for her that two women can parent quite well without a daddy, and she's seen the boys fly – that's the word she used. She said she didn't care who we were because we were clearly right for the boys.'

What both Ian and Fliss expressed to me, separately, was the fact that as gay adopters, they hadn't felt the same need or desire to have their own children. One of the exercises that potential adopters have to do is imagine their fantasy birth child, and then say goodbye to them. In a workshop Ian was asked to do the same: 'I remember looking around the room, thinking, "This must be so much harder for everyone else" because for us, it was never an option. We never had to try to have our own child, so I've always thought the adoption route was much easier.'

Fliss echoed this sentiment when she told me that she felt adoption wasn't considered a 'second choice' for same-sex couples as it possibly was for heterosexuals. 'I also think that some of my heterosexual adopter friends feel a sense of loss of the perfect family they couldn't have and so feel disappointed to have to deal with some of the issues they do, having adopted,' she says. 'One friend said that if they'd had their own then they wouldn't have had to, "Put up with this just to have a family." This was our first choice, not our last resort, so I think that changes how we approached it and feel about it.'

* * *

Ever since the first legislation on adoption in 1926, the law has allowed single people to adopt, as well as married couples. During the interwar years single men were allowed to adopt boys under 21, and girls with permission from the court, and single women could adopt boys or girls. Some unmarried mothers adopted their own illegitimate children to make them legitimate: the writer Rebecca West, for example, adopted her son Anthony with H.G. Wells in 1929. In *A Child for Keeps*, Dr Keating writes that figures from the Home Office show that in 1950, 28 single males and 155 single women adopted non-related children that year (out of a total of 8,259 adoptions). However, in an early edition to a guide for adoptive parents in 1969, its author, Jane Rowe, said that, 'It seems foolish to take a child from one single woman and give him to another.' Given the climate of the 1950s and 1960s, this statement was probably not unreasonable.

That climate has changed over the past few decades but the idea for the adoptive family to reflect the two-parent 'natural' family has been an enduring one. The conventional mum-and-dad family unit had been considered not only normal but advantageous for adopted children, the reasoning being that since the children are already vulnerable because of their past experiences, they should not have further obstacles put in their way by placing them in an unconventional set-up.

But adoption isn't conventional, or 'natural' – adoptive families are different, by virtue of the fact that they are brought together and created. So why use the 'norm' of a two-parent family as a standard setter?

Meanwhile the number of single-parent families has risen over the past few decades – according to figures published by BAAF in 2015, nine per cent of children were adopted by single parents during the year ending March 2014. The trend towards older motherhood continues and many single women who want a child have no need to turn to marriage for financial security.

The idea of being a single parent has never daunted Roxanne, 46. 'A lot of my family members are single mums, as were a lot of my friends,' she says. 'So it didn't frighten me in the least.

'The thought of living my life without children was a far greater fear.'

Roxanne adopted her 'energetic, loving, intelligent' daughter, Tamara, now ten, in 2007. Chatty, buoyant and with an easy laugh, Roxanne had led a busy, London life. She worked hard in her civil service job in middle management with the Home Office and enjoyed an active social life.

'I was the sort of person who, if someone said, "Rox, what are you doing tonight?" I'd be, "Right, I'm coming!" I worked long, hard hours, up until 11 or 12 at night, and often at weekends, so I played hard. I did my own thing – I loved my soap operas, I had lie-ins until whatever time I wanted. My friends were like, "Rox, that's all going to change with parenthood."'

She tells me that for as long as she can remember, she'd always wanted to be a mum. But continued problems with endometriosis coupled with the fact that she wasn't in a stable, long-term relationship made having children difficult. Unwilling to go down the fertility treatment route, she signed up to adopt.

'It was a second option, in comparison to having a birth child,' she admits. 'Now I wouldn't change it for the world, but it was making good out of a bad situation.'

Being black African-Caribbean worked to her advantage – her local social services were 'delighted' to have a black woman come forward – but there were concerns over her long working hours as well as the fact that she had a boyfriend at the time who wasn't going to play the role of father.

'They couldn't understand why we weren't looking to go down the aisle together, or live together, even though we'd been seeing each other for a few years. I understood the need to check him out, but my patience did begin to run out,' she says. In fact, it's one of the reasons why she now sits on adoption panels – to defend those who might not be in conventional relationships because, 'That's real life.'

Wary of what she might have to deal with as a single parent, Roxanne set strict parameters in terms of the children she would consider – a healthy, black boy or girl under the age of two.

Her daughter, who came to live with her in February 2007, had been removed from the birth family and put in foster care when she was first born and although there may have been drugs 'in the mix', taken by the birth mother, she had no withdrawal symptoms. The transition from foster care to Roxanne was smooth – she called her Mum from day one. 'Although she called everyone Mum, it felt good to me,' laughs Roxanne. 'You take what you want from it.'

She describes her daughter as 'an absolute joy – funny and ahead of the game' and their relationship, though loving and open, can be volatile. 'We can clash.'

Support from her mum and extended family has helped her to cope but she struggles with the fact that all decisions rest with her. A year ago she decided to put the once-a-year contact her daughter has with her siblings and birth grandmother on hold because it didn't seem to be beneficial: 'I felt guilty as I knew her grandmother was committed [to the contact] but I had to think, "I can't deal with that guilt, I need to do what's right for her." Whether I've made the right or wrong decision, I don't know.'

At times she has also struggled with the responsibility of discipline – especially when Tamara, aged nine, went through a spell of temper tantrums.

'I'm usually quite jovial, and a few people at work

said, "Rox, what's up?" I was really worried, and lost my confidence.

'A few of them were experienced parents of girls, who talked to me and said, "She's probably hormonal, you have to adapt your parenting as they grow up, as they become people in their own right, but you also have to let them know who's boss."

'I missed having someone else there,' she admits. 'If there was someone with the same level of responsibility as me, we'd have been dealing with it together, batting it to each other. Instead I was thinking, "If she's kicking off like this now, what is it going to be like when she's a teenager, and has more control?" All her need is going to be focused on me, but also her anger.

'There had never been any contention in my house when I was growing up so it just wasn't something I was used to.

'Gradually my confidence came back and when I need to be stern, I'm stern. But I guess this is what parenthood is all about.'

In the earlier days (although not so much now) Tamara used to question Roxanne about not having a dad – usually at inopportune times. 'She threw me a question once, "What happened to my Dad? Is he dead?" just as we were rushing out of the house to drive somewhere. I said something along the lines of, "Not as far as I know" and then tried to normalise it by saying, "There are lots of children whose dads aren't around."

'I then started to make a right old mess of it, trying to make the distinction between a birth father, and a "Dad" who looks after you. I must have been going on as she turned round to me and said, "Mummy, aren't you meant to be concentrating on driving?" She'd probably switched off hours ago.'

The relationship she'd been in soon ended – 'My priorities changed, I was knackered and I didn't have the time to give him any attention' – but she hasn't ruled out future relationships: 'I have my own needs so it would be nice to have someone around, especially in the teenage years when I might need a bit of support. But I'm not looking for it and I'd have to handle it delicately. I think she'd see that person as a threat.

'Although sometimes she'll say, "Mummy, who have you kissed?" We went on a cruise once and there was a member of staff who was being friendly, who she decided to hook me up with, which was embarrassing.'

Roxanne would encourage anyone considering adoption on their own to 'Go for it' but be prepared for the lifestyle change, selective about the sort of children to consider and aware of the fact that there is more uncertainty in being a single adoptive parent than a single parent of a birth child, which she believes is tied in with a child's sense of identity. 'At least if they're with their birth family they know they're related to them, they can see the resemblance. Whereas an adopted child doesn't have that.'

Although she's often told her daughter looks like her. 'And when she's being stubborn, friends say, "And who's the mother?"' she laughs. 'I'm like, "Yeah, right!"'

* * *

Sir Martin Narey, government advisor on adoption and chair of the Adoption Leadership Board, which aims to drive through improvements in the adoption system in England, believes one of the defining characteristics of adopters is resilience – to get through the assessment process and to accept whatever is thrown at them. 'You have to have the ability to retain optimism through some pretty difficult times,' he tells me. 'The assessment process is pretty horrible and the experience of being told just how awful adoption might be – it puts a lot of people off.'

To face these challenges on your own requires, I think, superhuman strength and an absolute, unwavering commitment. I had Harry to pick me up whenever I fell; single adopters only have themselves to rely on.

Despite a strong desire to be a parent, and confidence in her capacity, 'to love a child I hadn't given birth to', Ellen, 54, had to abandon her dream to adopt – a decision she still, occasionally, struggles with.

I enjoy talking to Ellen – she's honest, funny and reminds me of a lot of women I know. I'm also sure her story reflects many other single women who have tried to have a family.

When she was 39, Ellen, who was married at the time, suffered a miscarriage. She split up from her husband shortly afterwards and a couple of years later, having decided to have a child on her own, she fell pregnant with donor sperm. Sadly, various medical complications meant that she couldn't carry the baby to term and she had to have a termination.

It was just after her 44th birthday that she started to look into adoption, signing up to an independent adoption agency.

'To be honest, when I look back I think I was utterly unrealistic,' says Ellen, who works as a management consultant and lives in the Southwest with her partner. 'But being in my mid-forties, I felt I'd had lots of independent life. There's an expression which Nigella Lawson once used, which was something along the lines of, "When you become a parent you cease to be the picture and become the frame". And I was fed up with being the picture.

'That said, going through the occasionally bizarre process of being approved, I had an almost mad level of partying!' she adds. 'I embarked on a no-strings relationship with a guy who I was working with at the time – although it was all very above board – and had a lot of fun. I'm sociable and extrovert but I was never a wild party animal, but I had a few times when I'd still be dancing on a Friday night at two in the morning, thinking, "This is going to have to stop,"' she says, laughing.

Like Roxanne, Ellen felt that as a single woman she was subject to unnecessary scrutiny when it came to her love life. In her case, her social worker thought the fact that she'd had three previous long-term relationships was quite a significant number. 'That's the only time I snapped in the process,' she remembers. 'I said, "Here's what you need to know – I'm having sex on quite a regular basis. If it becomes serious, I'll let you know about it, but it won't. And of course if you want to do a search for all the drugs in the flat, start underneath the sink." He laughed, and it wasn't mentioned again.'

She liked the adoption agency, got on with her social worker and didn't, at any stage, feel she was being discriminated against for being single although, 'They were clear to me about the fact that being a single woman puts you further down the chain in terms of how local authorities and other agencies placing children might perceive me.' The fact that she wouldn't necessarily be their first choice was, she says, 'a clear message'.

In 2005, when she went to panel, everything was in place – she'd saved enough money to take six months off work and had rallied a strong support network, including her parents and friends. To her shock, and her social worker's horror, she was turned down. 'They didn't feel there was enough evidence that I'd be able to cope. My guess is that, being a single woman, they wanted a belt-and-braces approach.'

Undeterred, they went back to panel a couple of months later and she was approved to adopt one child, up to the age of six.

The first child she was almost matched with – Hayley, a seven-year-old girl who was meeting all her developmental milestones – fell through. The girl's social workers had been delighted with Ellen. 'They said, "You'll be perfect for this little girl" and I got a call from my social worker, saying, "You're going to be a mum!" I was massively excited. Then it all went very quiet. A week later, I got a call from my social worker, saying, "I don't know how to tell you this, but they've matched the little girl with someone else."'

It transpired Hayley's foster carers didn't believe that a single woman should adopt her. 'Apparently the foster father said, "She needs a dad – she must have a dad" so they wavered. They looked at the next people on the list, a couple, and accepted them.'

Ellen burst into tears when she was told the news, and then felt very angry at the social workers for what she considered to be their 'staggering ineptitude'. Shortly afterwards she was asked to consider two sisters, aged five and seven. 'Looking back, I think, "God almighty, how would I have managed two kids as a single woman?" But I signed up for it.'

Deciding she'd move back to the West Midlands once the children had been placed with her, to be near her mum for support, Ellen put her house on the market and secured a job transfer. Meanwhile, the girls' birth parents (who had been young drug users) had come back on the scene. There was already an arrangement in place for annual contact with the girls' maternal grandmother, who had been a strong figure in their lives, but now a request was made for regular contact with the birth parents as well.

'I pulled out,' says Ellen. 'The situation had morphed into something completely different and I felt I was going to sign up to be a foster carer, or a caretaker, rather than a parent. I was very sad to do it, it was a really hard decision, but to be honest, I think I needed a breather.

'Throughout my late thirties and up until my mid-forties I'd been trying to have a child, largely on my own, and I suddenly thought, "I can't do this." It was so hard and I felt very guilty, but I think I'd run out of energy. The whole process, both emotionally and financially, of pregnancy loss, spending thousands to get pregnant, of going through the adoption process, it had been too much.'

Taking what she thought was going to be a short break, Ellen never returned to the adoption process.

'I've often thought, "I wish I'd just taken a breather and carried on," as by now I would have had a child. But it's easy to replay a different story in your mind.'

Instead she met her current partner, with whom she now lives, and got on with her life. She can now look back on her desire to have a child with clarity and honesty, and without too much regret.

'Part of the reason I didn't return to it (when I might have done) was that I was nearing 50 and thought, "Am I really going to do this on my own?" I was desperate for a child, and thought I couldn't live without one, but as I got older I'm not sure I could have done it,' she admits.

Even so, although the thought of having a baby was 'terrifying', when she first met her partner she didn't use contraception. 'It was a case of waiting for the fat lady to sing and finally leave the stage.'

But is she sorted and happy now?

'Absolutely,' she says. 'I have a lot to be grateful for.'

Chapter Six

It was a warm day but I couldn't stop shivering. My jaw ached from clenching it and I wish I'd worn socks. I was meeting my son for the first time, a prospect so overwhelming that my body had gone into shock.

That morning we had driven up to the seaside town in the Northeast where Gabriel lived with his foster carers, Bill and Mary. They had looked after Gabriel since he was a baby and had grown to love him. Soon we'd be taking him away.

After a few minutes his foster father, Bill, came to the door with Gabriel in his arms. He'd just woken up from a nap and refused to open his eyes. His arms were wrapped tightly around Bill's neck and he wouldn't say hello. My first instinct was to reach out and touch him – stroke his olive skin, ruffle his short, soft hair, tickle his legs. I wanted him to put his arms around my neck, to make him laugh and kiss his cheeks – I didn't expect my reaction to feel so physical.

We filed into a cosy living room as the foster carers, their son and daughter and two social workers – Gabriel's and ours – settled in sofas and armchairs. We sat on the floor. In the photographs of that day I'm sitting awkwardly and wearing an embarrassed smile. We were there to observe and be observed – it was impossible not to feel on trial. Gabriel was a bit under the weather with a cold: he had a streaming nose and his green T-shirt had a big, wet patch down the front. For most of the time he ignored us, sticking close to Bill and Mary. 'He's not usually like this,' Mary kept saying apologetically.

We watched as he ate his lunch daintily, and played with the present we'd bought him: a big, red, wooden London bus. We'd spent hours in Hamleys, pondering over what felt like a hugely symbolic gift – our first. I put on my best children's TV presenter voice as I took out all the little passengers and lined them up. He knocked them over and wandered off. We were shown a photo album of pictures of Gabriel as a baby, including ones with his birth mother. A handsome woman with a good, strong face, she held her baby tightly and they looked close. I wondered how much she was going to haunt me. He was smiling in every picture – he must have come out of the womb smiling.

We stayed for an hour and as we were leaving Gabriel went off into the kitchen with his foster mother and came back with presents. He gave Harry a Mars Bar; he gave me a bunch of flowers with a note. It read: 'To my new Mummy and Daddy'.

On the journey back we were so exhausted we couldn't speak. Harry had to pull into a lay-by and drink a can of Coke just to keep awake. A sense of unreality hung over us; we knew it had been a momentous meeting, but couldn't yet process its significance. We had been trying to create a family for eight years and this was the culmination of all our efforts: a stifled, awkward encounter between strangers. I could only take it in incrementally – I was drawn to him; that was enough for now.

The first meeting is easily one of the most defining moments of any adoption. Not all mothers feel instant love when they give birth, but there must be an element of recognition, a sense of pride in your part in the baby's creation. Adoptive parents have to wait for love to come.

'The notion that you can acquire a child without going through all the birth stuff is quite weird,' says my friend Vicky, who adopted her daughter when she was 18 months old. 'If you've given birth, by the time you've got a two-year-old then two years have gone into creating that relationship. But people like us can go and get a two-year-old and instantly become parents. It's quite odd.'

Pregnant women have a nine-month gestation period in which they can make practical and emotional adjustments for their baby's arrival. Bedrooms are decorated, buggies bought and shops are scoured for clothes. Hormones kick in and the nesting instinct is alert and alive. They can wear their bump with pride and be celebrated for it. Until we had met Gabriel, we couldn't really prepare so our preparation for his arrival was rushed and ad-hoc. I'd furtively, almost superstitiously, bought bits and pieces from a couple of recent work trips – a few wooden animals from Africa, some paper kites and an embroidered bedspread from Pakistan – but there were no buggies in the hallway or safety catches on the cupboard doors. Gingerly, we began to decorate his room, a tiny box next to our bedroom just large enough to swing a cat in. We squeezed in a cot, donated by a friend, and an armchair.

At first I felt uneasy having him at such close quarters – I'd look at the door and imagine a child asleep – or crying – behind it. 'He's going to be close to you wherever he is, so you might as well get used to it,' my friend Susan pointed out. And, of course, as soon as he came home I was relieved to have him sleeping near us.

That week Harry and I took a trip to Mothercare and spent a couple of hours test-driving pushchairs, looking at linen for his cot and tiny bath towels with hoods. Finally we were allowed to indulge our fantasies and buy the things we'd craved, which felt indulgent and also slightly illicit. I got out my childhood wooden toys from storage, bought some paint and spent hours with a tiny brush patching up the little men who sat on a wonky roundabout. I filled his shelves with my ancient, tatty picture books and imagined reading them to him. We stuck pictures on the wall and made our own alphabet frieze in an arts-and-crafts frenzy of colour photocopying and laminating. The only thing we couldn't buy were clothes – we'd been told that the possessions he brought with him were sacrosanct, and that he'd need as many familiar things around him as possible. His clothes would smell like home.

* * *

Two weeks after our first meeting we set off for his hometown, where we would spend an 'introduction' week together, taking him out on a 'getting to know you' exercise.

The day before we left, we had a party to celebrate. For once, there were children running around the house and I didn't feel sad: we were becoming part of the club.

The following morning we drove to the bungalow we'd hired in an isolated spot overlooking a mudflat estuary, with the North Sea beyond and only a few other crumbling cottages for company. When the sun shone it had an eerie beauty, which quickly turned bleak on cloudy days. The bungalow itself was like a mad old aunty – rickety, eccentric and ramshackle, with few home comforts. But, strangely, there was a magnificent hot tub on the veranda, which we jumped into with the emergency bottle of champagne we'd brought from home. As I sat and watched ocean liners cross the horizon it seemed a suitably surreal start to an extraordinary experience.

The thing that struck me the most when we arrived for the first day at Bill and Mary's on that May morning in 2004 was the noise. Gabriel had woken up at his usual time of 4am and had been up for five hours, showing no signs of slowing down. Wearing a babygro and slippers, with a dummy stuck firmly in his mouth, he looked like a manic Teletubby as he ran in and out of the garden. It was decided he needed some exercise so we set off for the nearby park with an awkward enthusiasm – we didn't want to trespass onto Mary and Bill's territory and they tried to be sensitive and step back, encouraging Gabriel to walk with us, but most of the time he refused. Who could blame him? Harry handled it all with a natural ease – he chased Gabriel around and lifted him up onto his shoulders. I pushed Gabriel on a swing, my face stuck in a rictus grin. Even my 'Whhheeeees!' sounded a little fake. I looked at my watch and it was still only 10:30am – only a few hours had passed but it felt like a whole day.

Back at the house, Mary suggested I change Gabriel's nappy. My heart sank: I had an audience and didn't know where to start. Clearly an old hand, Gabriel was co-operative and uncomplaining, despite my initial clumsiness. I quite enjoyed my first parenting rite of passage. In fact, I never found changing his nappy abhorrent, perhaps because, not having given birth or breastfed, it was the closest I ever got to the full-on baby experience.

Although Bill and Mary couldn't have been more welcoming or helpful we still felt under scrutiny, so we asked if we could take Gabriel into town. Pushing his buggy for the first time felt hugely symbolic – but also potentially hazardous. I was in charge of a pram without a licence and unaware of the Highway Code. How do you cross a road between two parked cars without the buggy getting run over? Who has right of way on the pavement? And why did I feel like a middle-aged Vicky Pollard?

I wasn't a natural, nor were we prepared. It was a blistering hot day and Gabriel had no sun protection, or lunch. Suddenly filled with a sense of purpose, we roamed the busy streets looking for a sun hat and sausage roll. We'd been told it was a snack he particularly liked and we wouldn't rest until we found one, no matter that he'd fallen asleep. We dived into Marks & Spencer and Harry headed off towards the food section. 'Don't leave me,' I hissed. 'What if he wakes up? I won't know what to do!' I stood frozen to the spot, willing him to stay asleep until Harry got back.

We had that afternoon off. It was still hot so we sought refuge in a beautiful landscaped park, sitting on a bench underneath a huge magnolia tree. Relieved that we were on our own, not having to perform or prove ourselves, I lay down and watched the small white clouds scud across the sky.

For much of the week I felt exhausted, stressed and woefully inadequate. Gabriel was friendly and adaptable – he never cried, and he didn't complain. For the first time ever I had to learn how to communicate with someone who only had ten words in their vocabulary and the attention span of a gnat. But he knew how to put those words to their best use – 'Again!' '*Me!*' 'Here!' 'Again!' – and although not yet two, he could move fast.

One night, when we got back to the cottage after a day out with Gabriel, tired and sunburnt, I threw up. I blamed it on mild sunstroke but really I was in a state of panic. I was shocked at how tired I was. I'd been trying so hard to make Gabriel like me that I was exhausted with the effort, as well as the fatigue that comes naturally with looking after a child.

After little sleep filled with nightmares, I woke the next morning with fear and dread. By 8am we were at Mary and Bill's house, the TV blaring out while I sat sheepishly in an armchair. 'Ros isn't feeling too good,' said Harry, explaining my quietness. 'When you're looking after children there's no room to feel ill,' Mary pointed out. 'You just have to get on with it.' 'Cheers,' I thought.

I resolved that day not to try too hard: Gabriel would have to accept me as I was, not as some over-enthusiastic children's entertainer, which is how I'd felt. We went for a long walk in the countryside by a river, put down a rug and fed some ducks. Unusually quiet, Gabriel kept stroking our faces, as if trying to fathom us out. Photographs from that day show us looking warily tender but I was in a deep, dark hole, wracked with anxiety. My thoughts turned catastrophic: 'Harry is much better at this than I am. We're going to split up. He'll stay with Gabriel and I'll have to leave.' These weren't fears I could voice – at least, not in front of Gabriel. Even I was mature enough to realise that, at that moment his needs were greater than mine. But it struck me, not for the first time, that our lives really would never be the same again.

That evening, Mary suggested we give Gabriel his bath and put him to bed. I'd never bathed a child before and it felt intensely nurturing and intimate, wrapping him in a big, warm towel, rubbing cream into his dimpled brown skin. We both stayed with him until he fell asleep, sitting next to his cot and holding his hand through the bars. I felt the first stirrings of love.

But by the morning my pounding heart had returned. That afternoon we were driving back to London and so we were making the most of our last morning, arriving at the foster carers' by 6am. We were desperate to get out. Bill and Mary had been trusting but reserved, handing over the reins but at the same time reluctant to surrender authority. The evening before, when Gabriel was demanding his tea, Bill had said, 'There you go – you can make him an omelette.' But he had followed us into the kitchen and stood over Harry while he whisked an egg: he was their boy and we had a long way to prove that we could look after him. I don't know how they were able to bear it.

We drove to a seaside resort. Not yet 7am, the streets were deserted. Desperate for a coffee, we walked along the front and stared plaintively through the windows of a greasy spoon. Taking pity on us, the owner, still in her dressing gown, opened up early. 'He's lovely, isn't he? What a beautiful boy,' she cooed over Gabriel in his buggy. I couldn't join in; I felt he didn't belong to me and could take no credit for his loveliness. She began asking us questions. What was his name? How old was he? Where did we live? I started to panic. What if she asked us something we didn't know how to answer? Like, 'When did he get his first teeth?' Or worse still, 'He doesn't look English — where's he from?' What if she knows his birth family and starts piecing things together? We wolfed down our toast and made a quick exit, like fugitives on the run with a stolen child.

When we dropped him off later that day to drive back home, I could tell Harry was sad. I was confused. 'I'll miss him,' he said, as featureless countryside sped by on the motorway. Meanwhile I was terrified – like a parachute jumper waiting in line, I couldn't make the leap. I felt weak and cowardly, threatened and anxious – all the things I knew I couldn't be if Gabriel was to have a safe and secure home. Concerned but exasperated, Harry told me to ring our social worker, Satwinder.

'I can't do this,' I sobbed down the phone. 'It's not him – it's me.' He told me my reaction was perfectly normal. I was reassured; sitting next to Harry, all calm and composed, I'd felt like a freak. 'It would be different if you said there was a problem with Gabriel,' he said, 'but there isn't. You like him so it will be all right.' It was true: I did like him. He was good fun, confident, easy-going and beautiful, and he'd put his trust in us, two strangers. It was going to be a huge leap of faith, but I still wasn't sure how much of that I had.

The last two days of the introduction week were spent in our flat. Bill and Mary brought Gabriel to stay with us while they stayed in a local hotel. He adapted immediately – and so did I. The crippling anxiety that had gripped me for the last week slowly began to lift. I was on home territory in a familiar environment; I knew the local shopkeepers, I could find my way around the streets and sleep in my own bed. It was a relief bringing Gabriel into our home. He fitted far more comfortably into my world, it seemed, than I had in his.

After two days at our house we dropped Gabriel off at his foster carers' for his last weekend with them. It was a long round trip. We spent our last Saturday night as a childless couple in a McDonald's car park, eating Big Macs before hitting the motorway for our long journey home.

* * *

I can't remember much about the day we went to collect him, except that a lot of people cried. We turned up to be met by a full household – his foster carers and two of their children, Gabriel's social worker and a couple of the other foster children were waiting for us in the living room. Sensing the tension, Gabriel began to cry. Then his foster mother burst into tears and his foster father left the room. We set off quickly after hugs all round.

'We did our best to smile when he left,' wrote Mary in her diary entry that day, which she later sent to me to keep for Gabriel, 'but it was one of the hardest things we have had to do as foster carers. We loved you as our own.'

As we turned the corner I looked back to see them clumped in a small group, waving. Gabriel was coming to live with his 'forever' family but they were the only family he'd ever known – and we were taking him away from them.

Chapter Seven

I remember meeting up with a friend and her adopted two-year-old boy, who'd only been together for a few weeks, but behaved as if they'd known each other forever. He called her 'Mummy' and she rose magnificently to the role, anticipating his needs, second-guessing his moods and clearly relishing his company. I was staggered by her confidence – she pushed his buggy as if she owned the pavement. How did she do it? When I first became a parent my face was set in a permanent look of panic as if I wielded an invisible placard saying, 'I've no idea what I'm doing'.

I've never been pregnant, but I'm pretty sure that most mothers who give birth to their children form a bond as soon as they know they've conceived. By the time the baby has grown into a toddler, the bond has also grown and a relationship built on love, trust and familiarity has developed. You've had two years to nurture them when helpless; they've endeared themselves to you with their first smile, steps or tooth. When you adopt a toddler, however, you are entrusted with the welfare of a stranger: a bombastic, energetic, often unreasonable force of nature with its own personality and strong ideas about how to do things. As Kate Figes writes in her book, *Life After Birth*: 'If nature had given a newborn baby the ability to make the same demands as a child of 12 months older, the mother would be devastated and the levels of infanticide would probably soar.' When I look at toddlers now I'm amazed I didn't run around the flat screaming, 'What have I done?'

Harry and I had spent eight and a half years yearning for a child. Then one came storming into our life like a small tornado. Overnight, my life changed in more ways than I'd ever imagined. I never finished a conversation or put my needs first; I mastered the art of crawling on all fours, pushing small cars mumbling 'brum, brum' and miming the actions to nursery rhymes; I spoke with unnatural levels of enthusiasm and suffered unprecedented levels of tiredness; I rarely socialised but would look forward with relief to my first glass of wine at 6pm, sharp. I had more patience than I'd thought, but also discovered a bad temper; I couldn't pop out for a pint of milk without him or leave the house without a rucksack of child-friendly emergency supplies and provisions; my world shrank to a mile radius, where I became intimate with every café and swing park; I was on first name terms with the ducks and moorhens and measured my days in minutes not hours, punctuated by naps and snacks (his, not mine). Everything took a lot longer than it used to.

It was, in short, a crash course in parenting and I hadn't

read the manual. We had, however, been given a list from social services of the sort of information we'd need to know about Gabriel before he came to live with us: What time did he wake up? What frightens him? What frustrates him and what makes him smile? What are his favourite foods? Or music? Does he have a bedtime ritual? What does he sleep in? Does he suffer car sickness? What clothes does he feel comfortable wearing? Which is his favourite toy? Does he like cuddling?

We were also advised on small details which we'd never have considered ourselves – for example, to use the same brand of washing powder as his foster carers so he'd be wearing a familiar smell; to not change his wardrobe (however strong the urge to kit him out in the clothes we were desperate to dress him in); to not overwhelm him in the first few days with too many new visitors (including very keen grandparents) or exhaust him with too many outings. We took with us from the foster home a bit of Mary's perfume, so that he'd have another comforting scent, and a CD of Ronan Keating, which she'd play to send him to sleep.

There were three things from his foster home to which he became passionately attached as soon as he arrived, clinging to them like a lifeline: a pristine white blanket, which he called 'Gankit', a small cuddly leopard, which I named 'Tiger' in a moment of panic, and a dummy. Gankit is now a grey, smelly scrap of a thing and Tiger has seen better days, but I, too, have an unnaturally strong attachment to them. The dummy upset my middle-class sensibilities and the health visitor warned us that it could impede his speech (like Maggie in *The Simpsons*, he was

127

never without it) but we soon wised up to the fact that depriving him of it would be tantamount to abuse. We would pack these three essential items every time we left the house – along with clean nappies, raisins, rice cakes, pieces of cut-up apple, clean trousers and socks, wet wipes, a picture book and two spare dummies.

As soon as we'd turned the corner from Bill and Mary's house on the day we brought him home, Gabriel fell asleep, and stayed asleep until we reached our house. We guessed it was his way of coping with the emotional upheaval. He has no recollection of that day, and I find it difficult to imagine how he must have felt, removed from the home he'd grown up in and the family he loved, to live with two strangers in a different house with all its unfamiliar smells, textures, colours and sounds. Looking at photographs of that day, we all seem ridiculously happy. It was gloriously sunny so we got out the paddling pool and chased Gabriel around the garden with a watering can as he shrieked with laughter. That night, after his bath, he fell asleep on Harry's lap.

We were told to expect a spectrum of emotions from sad to excitable, to confused, angry and depressed. He might also be on his best behaviour so as not to displease, and depending on how he coped with the rejection he must have felt, be either clingy and insecure or independent and distant. For some children, we were told, being moved from their foster home was akin to a loss by death: our little boy was in mourning.

Over the next few weeks and months, he displayed all of these emotions and behavioural patterns, and more. All compounded by the fact that he was a two-year-old with typical toddler traits. But what made it easier for us, and continues to do so now, is that he's a happy boy with a lightness of spirit who loves to laugh.

* * *

Harry and I had decided to take six weeks off work together, with the plan that I'd take a further two months off, after which I'd go back to work and he would stay at home for the following two months. Looking back now it seems a ridiculously short amount of time but it was all we could afford. For those first few weeks we lived in a bubble – the concept of work, or a social life, or any topic of conversation that wasn't about Gabriel felt alien. We ignored advice about not taking him on too many outings and in the first week alone spent a day in a park's paddling pool, a day in town to buy a buggy (where Harry quickly learnt how to change a nappy in a tiny Starbucks' toilet), toured the Tate Modern and one morning attempted to take part in a music workshop for babies and toddlers. As Harry and I bashed away enthusiastically on triangles and drums with all the other eager parents and children, trying to fit in, Gabriel made a break for it. He just didn't want to know – and who could blame him? Who were those crazy people making him play percussion? But still I asked myself what was to become a constant question: 'Is that normal?' As a friend with three sons wisely advised, nothing was 'normal' with two-year-old boys.

'They're all full-on at that stage,' she reassured me in an email. 'Total mobility and not much understanding of things.' But that took a while to understand. In those early days I was on the lookout for signs of trauma, manifesting itself in odd behaviour. I didn't know that most toddlers are incapable of behaving in any way other than odd. I clung to a fact that I'd gleaned from a book another adoptive mother had given me: that a child placed with a family before they were two years old stood a better chance of settling than one older than two. The fact that Gabriel was just shy of his second birthday was proof enough for me that he'd be OK.

What I did feel immediately comfortable with was the physicality of him, being so close to this small person with his perfect body, bathing him, dressing him and changing his nappies. But it took months, even a year, before Gabriel was completely at ease with intimacy. I wanted to envelop him in hugs and for him to throw his arms around me and while he could be affectionate, he didn't like to be smothered. The feel of flesh on flesh seemed to make him uncomfortable. I was expecting too much, of course: he didn't know me, and had no reason to trust me yet, but it didn't stop me from looking for clues.

After four weeks we had what felt like a minor breakthrough. I was sitting in the kitchen of a friend's house with her one-year-old daughter on my lap. Gabriel came into the room and, seeing us, insisted on climbing up too. 'I know it's silly but it meant a lot to me,' I later wrote in my diary. 'It shows he has some attachment.'

After he'd been with us for four months, Gabriel had to have his MMR (mumps, measles and rubella) injection. For a day it made him feel a bit under the weather and, for what felt like the first time, clingy. He wanted to get as close to me as he could, sitting on my lap and burying his head in my chest. Now all I have to do is look at him in

ROSALIND POWELL

a certain way and he'll say, 'I know what you're after – a cuddle.' Back then it felt like a rare gift.

It was with a sense of caution that we slowly introduced him to our family and friends. Harry's parents couldn't wait to meet him, although his stepdad worried about being accepted by Gabriel. 'Will he call me granddad?' he asked, eager to step into the role. My mum, who had been virtually stalking us, had to wait almost a week before she was allowed to come round. 'I was so apprehensive when I was finally invited to meet him, and so relieved that I liked him so much,' she says now. 'I can honestly say that within minutes, I fell in love.' Within minutes she had also burst into tears. When Gabriel met my sister, a day later, he burst into tears. By the end of his first month he'd met an astonishing 23 adults and 15 children, all for the first time.

When we celebrated his second birthday we were touched by the outpouring of affection and acceptance that came from friends and family who hadn't even met him yet. His birthday cards were symbolic of his past and future, and of the handover in care. 'To my darling Grandson, from your Grandma with all my love,' wrote my mum. Bill and Mary wished him 'all the happiness in all the world' and said they'd be thinking of him always. 'Keep safe,' they added, no longer the custodians of his safety. Their card made me cry. I also thought of his birth mother, and how she must have been feeling. In my diary I keep a picture of Gabriel from that day: he's standing in a puddle next to the new bicycle we bought him, wearing a diffident smile.

Sleep and time became an obsession for me. Gabriel was an early riser – 5am at his worst, 6:30am if we were lucky – and Harry and I would take turns in getting up with him. We'd sit on the sofa, comatose, looking out on the eerie twilight world of nightshift workers and insomniacs, and watch *Hairy Maclary* or *Pingu*. By 7am we were in the park – luckily, we lived opposite one – and by 9am we'd run out of things to do. The day stretched out ahead, and I felt compelled to fill every minute. Sometimes we'd just roam the streets, pushing him in his buggy. The local Somerfield became a regular stop-off, often the focal point of the day. Because of his energy levels I was more comfortable with him outdoors than inside, where he could run wild and free.

'When does he have his quiet moments?' asked my mum, who had brought up two girls, which, I discovered, was a completely different parenting experience. 'Why can't he just sit and read a book?' I'd ask myself as Gabriel charged around the flat, kicking balls, smashing building blocks and shouting 'HAR-RY!' every few minutes.

His vocabulary was limited to words such as 'gone', 'here', 'ball', 'no' and 'Oh, Gawd', which was our little joke. Two weeks later, he'd added 'cup of tea', 'itchy', 'throw away' and 'can't do it'. But his favourite was 'Harry', which he'd call us both, repeatedly, and particularly loudly in swing parks. It was six weeks until he called us Mummy and Daddy. Maybe we had to earn the title. In the meantime I felt amused, embarrassed – especially in front of other mums – and, at times, hurt. Which was completely irrational, of course, but both Harry and I were trying to win his affection and at times I felt as if I was losing out.

I was very up and down in those early days. I'd veer from the joy and excitement of having a child, relishing the small moments such as pushing him in the buggy, making him laugh or cuddling him on my lap as I read him his bedtime story to the milestone ones such as when he called me Mummy for the first time. Or I'd feel exhausted, anxious or depressed. Harry and I also argued in a way that we'd never done before. Our lives had changed overnight and we were living in a highly charged environment compounded by lack of sleep. I either felt closely bonded through the shared experience, or isolated and cut off from him. We were used to each other's undivided attention – now we had to share it. But I also sensed a competitive edge to our relationship: we were both trying to win the affection of this little boy. 'I think he's enjoying it more than me, and doesn't analyse things in the same way, and that makes us frustrated with each other at times,' I emailed to a friend. 'I get annoyed with him because he won't acknowledge the difficulties, or admit to his vulnerabilities, and he gets annoyed with me for thinking about it all too much. We're both trying to bond with this little boy, and get him to love us, so we're on our own separate missions to form a relationship with him.'

A few weeks had passed and I remember my mum talking about how much she loved Gabriel, and asking me if I felt the same. But I didn't know how to answer that. I felt totally committed to him, and protective of him, and knew without doubt that he was our child but I didn't know if I would define that yet as love. After two weeks I wrote in my diary, 'I love him today.' I knew that love would come but there were times when I'd think, 'What if it doesn't?' Gabriel, in turn, wasn't always fully at ease with us. He wasn't uncomfortable as such, but we sensed he was just as comfortable with strangers. We'd been warned that this was a common trait with adopted children: they were so used to being cared for by different people that they found it difficult to form bonds with individuals. And that over-confidence in adopted children could be a sign of lack of attachment. Although Gabriel hadn't had many carers, we sometimes felt that he'd happily go off with anybody who asked him. In fact, I think he was just sociable.

Having shared our lives for a number of years now, I can spot the similarities between us. Like Harry, Gabriel points with his middle finger. He can raise one eyebrow, like me. And people who don't know us as a family often think he looks like Harry. One mother at his old nursery actually thought he looked like my mum.

But at the beginning I'd look at Gabriel and not be able to see either Harry or myself in him. We didn't share a gene pool and so we had no genetic influence over him. I couldn't be reassured by similarities or common traits – physical, emotional or psychological – he has Harry's patience, my sense of humour, my dad's hands, etc. This was of no concern to Harry, who claimed (and still does) that he didn't 'believe in genes.' For him, in the nature versus nurture battle, nurture won every time whereas sometimes I'd look at Gabriel and wonder, 'Who are you? And how are you going to turn out?' Although I guess you could argue that any birth parent could think that of their child.

Looking back, I feel embarrassed by some of my ridiculous expectations and high ideals, all borne out of ignorance, I suppose. I really didn't understand why he couldn't be quieter at times, or more affectionate, or less energetic. Or why his vocabulary wasn't wider; his demands less constant. And while Gabriel could be as challenging as the next toddler – stubborn, demanding, loud and unreasonable – he was extraordinary in his adaptability and sociability, his easy laugh, his independence and resilience. I think I only really fully appreciate that now. Sometimes I wish I could have some of that time with him again, with the greater understanding I have now. But maybe I wouldn't do things differently. Besides, hindsight is a wonderful thing.

Friends have since told me that both Harry and I appeared relaxed, natural and in control, and that Gabriel settled in quickly. Even though we listened hungrily to the advice of friends who were experienced parents, they didn't have to regularly pop by and check we were coping. To the outside world, almost immediately we became a family but my feelings of inadequacy, of being a fake, made me extremely self-conscious. I'd make excuses for my incompetency, blurting out. 'He's adopted!' to anyone who would listen – dog-walkers in parks, shopkeepers, bus drivers.

I'd take him along to mother and toddler groups and feel left out of the gang. I'd compare my behaviour to the other parents and find mine lacking – I wasn't enthusiastic enough or confident that he was meeting his developmental milestones. Should he be able to build up bricks without knocking them down, wipe his own nose, or recite a poem? We didn't yet have that invisible bond; he didn't constantly return to me for reassurance. Instead we circled each other like strangers.

We never spoke down to Gabriel, or used baby talk, but

we couldn't be monotone either. My voice often sounded unnaturally high with a false level of excitement – 'Oooh, look at that!', 'Well done, good boy!', 'The wheels on the bus...', etc. It was easier when we could just let rip and act daft, run around in circles to the Benny Hill theme tune, patting his bottom; hide behind trees and fall over.

My sense of transparency wasn't helped by the insensitivity of strangers. My hairdressers were the worst. 'What blood's he got in him?' asked one girl as she washed my hair, with Gabriel sitting next to me. 'Where's his dad from?' another wanted to know. Once, when Harry and I were sitting outside a café with Gabriel in his buggy, we got chatting to an elderly couple. Looking at Gabriel, the man said, 'Well, he's certainly caught the sun, hasn't he?', which stunned us into silence. Five minutes later, still puzzling over this white couple with their brown baby, he said to Harry, 'It's funny, because his eyes are brown and both of yours are blue.' I suppose these remarks were innocent enough, but their insidious nosiness only helped make me feel even more self-conscious.

This was compounded by the fact that we were still under close scrutiny by the social services. Gabriel still didn't legally 'belong' to us: for him to become legally ours, we had to apply for an Adoption Order, the process by which legal ties between the birth parents and child are severed and full parental responsibility for the child is granted solely to the adoptive parents and still be regularly assessed. It made us feel judged, with an underlying unease that he could be taken away from us. He'd only been with us a few months when we had to take him to A&E after he'd fallen over and banged his head in Tumble

Tots. He'd been fine, but that evening he was sick and we were advised to get him checked out. As we nervously registered his details I was convinced the receptionist was eyeing us with suspicion and was about to alert the social services. Were we going to be branded unfit parents? It felt as if there was no room for mistakes or accidents.

Along with our visits from Satwinder, we had to go through official reviews – three altogether – during which our progress would be judged by three social workers, including our own. The first took place just weeks after Gabriel's arrival. His social worker noted in the report that, 'He was showing off a little but was very relaxed and comfortable in his environment.' It was also noted that, 'He was showing a very comfortable, warm interaction with both his mum and his dad and was sitting on his mum's lap for most of the time.' I remember the moment when Gabriel came waddling over to sit on me to be hugely significant: it was a very public gesture of affection, which showed we were doing something right. When measured, he was found to have grown half an inch – another good sign. His vocabulary had also expanded from the 33 words I'd logged at the beginning to 84, including 'digger', 'flamingo' (bizarrely) and the oft-used 'banged my head'.

Even the not-so-positive bits were encouraging. 'Because Gabriel had been such a very amiable, easy-going child it was quite a shock when on the fourth week, he started being aggressive; throwing things around; stopped being as affectionate as he had been,' said the report. But apparently I felt 'sufficiently confident' to deal with those challenges and wasn't, 'worrying the whole time if she is doing the right thing.'

I must have put on a good show because I was either quaking in my boots or filled with anger at Gabriel's sudden change of mood. After five weeks of exemplary behaviour, he became whingy, whiny and aggressive, hitting out at both Harry and me. Satwinder saw this as part of his grieving process and said that he was displaying classic behaviour given his circumstances. In fact, it was reassuring that he was reacting at all. We'd all been slightly concerned by his compliance – he hadn't once asked after Mary and Bill, or cried for them. When we decided to put a photograph of them up on the fridge, to remind him of them, he hit it with his dummy. Again this was seen as a positive – he was venting his fury at having been abandoned by them. Although, as I wrote in my diary, 'It's just difficult to see the grief when he hits out if his toast isn't ready on time.'

To me his behaviour, especially its unpredictability, felt like a deliberate campaign to grind me down. He could switch in a minute, going from our smiling, co-operative, easy-going little boy – which is when I sensed he felt secure, safe and confident about his place in the home and in our lives – to an all-controlling mini dictator. One morning he slapped me so hard in the face that I burst into tears. After a few weeks of being hit regularly every single day (always after not getting his own way) I began to think for the first time, 'What have I done?'

'It's relentless,' I wrote in my diary after the first week of having looked after him on my own. 'I feel that when I'm with Gabriel I have no control over the situation, that he rules everything. He keeps saying, "That way" in the park and then when you follow, he goes off in the opposite direction. He insists on pushing the buggy then abandons it. He screams when we leave the swings, or have to change his nappy, or when I take his uneaten dinner away. He demands everything, constantly – yellow dummy, *Pingu*, grapes, *Jungle Book*. And says, "Mummy, cuddle" when really all he wants is to be carried somewhere because he doesn't want to walk. I look at other mothers and they seem so much more in control. They seem to know what to do whereas I just feel like I'm drowning. I have a constant feeling of, "What do I do now? How do I respond to that? Will that send him off into another tantrum?" I'm beginning to seriously doubt whether I have the right stuff to do this. I'm not sure I do. I'm not sure I want to.'

He'd developed a high-pitched scream that he could keep going for quite a while. My worst, inherent fears came to the fore, worrying he'd turn into 'someone aggressive who can only relate through violence'. I read that now and am surprised that I could have so easily misinterpreted common or garden toddler behaviour, or that I could have been so catastrophic. But then I knew nothing about toddlers. If I had that time again, I sometimes think now, would I do things differently? Feel differently? I like to think I would – but then again, it's easy to forget the sheer exhaustion and frustration that can come with looking after little kids.

To make matters worse, Gabriel's sleep pattern was very disturbed. Not only was he waking up at the crack of dawn, he wouldn't settle at night either. Harry or I would sit with him on our laps, listening to nursery rhymes, or holding his hand until he fell asleep. Then he'd wake in the early hours, crying. My lovely bedtime routine of bath, story, milk and then sleep had disappeared. I felt my evenings had been hijacked as well as my mornings. I became so preoccupied I began writing a log of his wake-up times. I was like a boarding school matron, registering lights on and off, unwavering in my determination that he should sleep in his cot and not in our bed, which other friends had done with their kids.

'Satwinder says it's part of the trauma cycle – I hope he's right,' I wrote. 'I can't be doing with this for weeks on end.'

I don't like the sound of myself in these diary entries: my frustration, apparent lack of understanding, patience or tolerance. Also, I feel sorry for us that I was so inflexible – we could have had a few lovely nights or mornings with him snoozing in our bed. I wish I knew then what I know now – that these things pass. I feel worse when I look at photographs of Gabriel taken around this time; Harry had begun to document him daily, and in each picture he looks so sad and lost, his eyes dark and unsmiling.

On a rational level I could understand that Gabriel had to cope with the trauma of being severed from his family and placed with another but he wasn't able to articulate any of it. Any big changes were hard for him – they still are. Without language, his moods and tantrums were the only way he could express himself: his sadness, anger or fear. But on an emotional level I struggled to deal with this child who had suddenly taken charge of my life with his tantrums and rage. I was used to being able to control things around me, but now things felt out of control; I also had nothing to compare it with.

At times I mourned my past: a weekend in Norfolk made me nostalgic for the times Harry and I used to go there together, alone. I planned a day's shopping trip with Sunita, and felt guilty for escaping my responsibilities, and then guilty for not feeling guilty enough; I even did a day's work during this time, an interview with the journalist John Simpson and his wife, Dee Kruger. We spent much of it talking about Gabriel, and when I got home, I discovered I'd forgotten to switch on my tape recorder for most of it: my brain was clearly scrambled. I didn't miss work and enjoyed the novelty of not having to do any, but I did wonder how I'd ever get back into it. My every waking moment was taken up with Gabriel, so how would I ever be able to concentrate on anything else ever again?

After a few weeks Bill, Mary and their family came to visit. When they arrived, Gabriel threw himself into Bill's arms, delighted to see them. Back at the flat he sat on their laps and they played with his ears, an old trick that made him laugh. He even fetched his favourite book, *Brown Bear*, and asked Bill to read it to him. When they left, a couple of hours later, he fell fast asleep, drained.

I felt conflicted about their visit: I could see it was good for Gabriel, but it reminded me of his past, a past that had nothing to do with us. I felt jealous of their bond and history with him. It was hard when I was trying to earn the right to call him my son, which I still struggled with saying (just as I still struggle with calling Harry 'my husband') – I found 'my boy' easier. I was also increasingly aware of just how much I loved him: I could feel it creeping through my bones.

The meeting was hard for Gabriel; it left him feeling tired, grumpy and distressed. I was angry with the social workers for advising us to meet up with them. What did they know? Who were they to tell us that it was for the best? They didn't have to deal with the fallout. To Harry and me it seemed almost a cruel exercise. He might not appreciate it now, Satwinder told us, but he would thank us for it when he was older, and we'd see the benefits. And we're just as grateful now to have kept up a relationship with the people who played a fundamental role in Gabriel's first two years.

* * *

Eventually the day arrived that I'd been dreading: Harry went back to work and I was left holding the baby. Filled with fear at the prospect of coping on my own, I booked a full and busy social diary for the pair of us. Rarely a day went by when we weren't with friends and their children.

We went to the library playgroup and the One O'Clock Club, to Tumble Tots and Baby Gym, Soft Play and the Tickle Monster. I'd pack for an expedition and take him to the Science and Natural History museums, Tate Modern and the South Bank, Kensington Palace Gardens and Richmond Park. I remember pushing him proudly down Sloane Street, him looking cool in a sheepskin coat, popping into the designer shops with my beautiful baby. I remember panicking in Patisserie Valerie, desperate to go to the loo and nervously leaving Gabriel with the waiter, wondering if he'd still be there when I got back. We had art and craft mornings with Sunita, rolling out huge stretches of wallpaper and stripping him down to his nappy so he could get covered in paint. There were afternoons in the park with my mum, feeding the ducks. I spent days with Susan and her two-year-old son Jack, taking them swimming and to the park. A few more words were added to his repertoire, as well as, 'Mummy do it.' I enjoyed not working, we had fun together: I had fallen in love.

We were beginning to take the shape of a 'normal' family, emotionally and practically, but not legally. After three months we took Gabriel to our house in Spain for the first time. He was still under a Full Care Order from the County Council, where he'd been born and fostered, and we had to have their written consent every time we left the country with him. Whenever we flew and went through Passport Control we felt like child smugglers, although we were only asked to produce evidence of our guardianship once, by a particularly officious airline worker. She was pleasant enough but we felt like criminals.

At the same time I was struggling with a sense of 'entitlement' when it came to being Gabriel's mother. It wasn't so much about *learning* to become a mother, it was about feeling I had the *right* to be one. I discovered my feelings were common to adoptive parents – well, according to one of the books I'd read. 'The issue of adoptive parents' rights to parent their children may seem moot on the surface,' reads one passage in *Real Parents, Real Children*, 'but parents often feel challenged in many ways. People will ask, "Don't you want children of your *own?*" or, in the case of interracial, intercultural or international adoption, "Are you being fair to the child by taking it away from its people?" Adoptive parents are often as vulnerable as their children when such comments are made.'

This would manifest itself in subtle ways. I remember watching a drama about the Asian tsunami of 2004, in which a mother was grieving the death of her five-year-old daughter, and accusing her husband of not having saved her. 'My baby,' she screamed, 'I've lost my baby!' I found it difficult to relate to, as I didn't feel I'd have the right to feel that way: I didn't own Gabriel, therefore he wasn't *my* baby. It's different now; he's very much my baby, and always will be (as I'm always telling him) – in fact, he's not going to be allowed to leave home. But even now I still find myself checking my legitimacy as a parent. If I feel nostalgic when watching little penguin toddlers waddling around in the park, or coo over a friend's baby, somewhere a voice is telling me, 'What do you know? You only cared for a small child for a fleeting moment!' But maybe that's how all parents feel.

I was also undergoing a slow transformation. As much as I'd struggled at times with Gabriel's moods, tantrums and demands, along with the everyday mundaneness of looking after a small child, I had discovered my inner earth mother and grown more confident. I had an overwhelming, almost physical need to carve out my role as chief nurturer in our family. I wanted to be the one to bathe, feed and clothe him; to look after him if he was ill, or comfort him if he was sad, to be his emotional guardian. I wanted Harry to play the hunter-gatherer, to be the 'dad' and kick a ball around, engage in a bit of rough and tumble, and leave the nurturing to me. In our relationship we had always shared things equally, without separately defined roles; now I wanted us to be equal but different. I felt resentful about all manner of things: the fact that I had to go back to work and couldn't be financially supported by Harry, and the fact that I'd been denied my 'natural' rights as a mother – to get pregnant, give birth, breastfeed. 'And now

I've been denied the chance to look after my child,' I wrote bitterly in my diary.

Harry was acquiescent – he allowed me to take control of bath-time and bedtime. My girlfriends were sympathetic. 'Of course you feel like that,' they'd say, 'you're his mother.' A few months later, wanting to explore my feelings further, I wrote a feature about it and was able to grill my friends. Without exception they admitted that they enjoyed being in charge, and while their partners were brilliant fathers and fully co-operative, they themselves made the final decisions. 'In most cases, women see themselves as the captain of the domestic childcare ship,' psychologist Oliver James told me, 'and the man is at best a first mate.' My friend Jo reassured me that my role would become even more defined as Gabriel grew older: I'd be the one to sort out nursery and school, homework and play dates, childcare, sick notes and dental appointments, and she was right.

Meanwhile Gabriel was blissfully unaware of the different roles I desperately wanted Harry and me to play, and was impervious to my efforts to make him notice. When he was about three we sat down one day to watch *Bambi* together. I'd been warned that he might cry at the bit when Bambi's mum gets shot, but he remained unmoved. 'Are you upset? There's no one to look after Bambi,' I said. 'Well, he's still got his Daddy,' he replied.

I couldn't argue with that.

As the day of my return to work loomed, I grew increasingly resentful, to the point where both Harry and I decided it would be better all round if I stayed at home for another month. But when the day came it was still hard going back. Being a full-time mother had, surprisingly, given me a huge sense of satisfaction and achievement. When the health visitor came round and said Gabriel was thriving, I'd taken full credit for it. 'I feel absolutely torn apart from him, and I can't bear it,' I wrote in my diary. 'I feel so jealous and possessive leaving him with Harry, but what can I do?'

Even the days when I worked at home weren't easy. Harry and Gabriel would go off to Soft Play together and I'd feel 'distant' from them – left out, in other words. I cried when he ignored me when I came in from work. He cried one morning when I left – which was horrible for him, but quite reassuring for me. I kept stewing on the fact that I'd only had three months at home with him on my own (having previously feared being left alone with him). Also, I was furious to find that Harry had reorganised all the kitchen cupboards. Like a big Tomcat, he'd marked his territory, or so it felt to me. We had a huge row, during which he demanded to be allowed to put Gabriel to bed a couple of nights a week. I gave in, realising my radical mothering campaign had to come to an end and that I'd been selfish. Harry is less vocal and analytical about parenting than I am, but he still had his own needs, which included the bonding rituals of bed- and bath-time.

* * *

With most adoptions, there is some contact with the birth family at some point. This can be direct contact, with face-to-face meetings between adopted children and birth parents or siblings. Or it can be indirect, or 'letterbox' contact between the adoptive and birth families, which is directed through the social services. When we were matched with Gabriel, we were offered the opportunity to have a one-off meeting with his birth mother, but she declined, and we were relieved. According to our social worker Satwinder that happened a lot.

'It's not because people don't care about the child they've lost, it's just that they can't deal with the reality of it,' he explained. 'People feel judged. "What if they don't like me? What if they think I've been a bad mother?" And adoptive parents on the other side are thinking, "What if they don't like us? Will they think we're stealing their baby?" There are always going to be two sides to every story, particularly in adoption, because the reality is, there usually are.'

I wondered at the rationale behind these meetings, which could surely only result in feelings of sadness and guilt on both sides. Who was it supposed to help? Of course, Gabriel may have benefited if we had met – we could have described his birth mother to him, brought her out of the shadows, given her shape, given him knowledge about his first days. But maybe it was just a fantasy harboured by the professionals not emotionally involved in the story.

I longed for the time when Gabriel could become legally ours, when we wouldn't have to deal with social services or social workers. 'It must have been so much easier in the old days,' I wrote in my diary, 'when you were just left to get on with it and allowed to claim your child as your own.'

But every year on his birthday I think of Gabriel's birth mother.

* * *

Life had begun to settle down into a routine. We found a wonderful nursery for Gabriel two days a week, while we shared the other three days between my mum and ourselves. I entered my busiest work year yet and discovered that I wasn't very good at multi-tasking – I was struggling with my juggling. I felt a good mother when I was with Gabriel on my own and had nothing else to think about, but became less tolerant and patient when I had to think about work too. Harry and I still struggled with time and identity issues. He suddenly wanted us to up sticks and move to Spain – an idea I thought was bordering on the insane. After long, heated discussions it transpired that his own latent anxiety about parenthood had expressed itself in a need to take flight: he was worried about us turning into Mr and Mrs Suburbia, with our lives predictably mapped out and governed by schools. But our most furious row was over his suggestion that he shared my office. Just the very thought induced a panic attack – I couldn't bear to give up my last bastion of privacy and space. This was where I came to escape, to just sit at my desk if I wanted to; I couldn't aimlessly ponder with someone else in the room.

'I don't think he likes me very much at the moment,' I wrote in my diary. 'He keeps giving me this hurt look. It feels like we're having difficulty loving each other. There's no intimacy – just irritation and grudges.' Looking back, it's obvious that, like any new parents, we were struggling with the extra demands being made of us, which left little time for ourselves, or each other. We'd never really argued like that before – and we haven't really since.

We went through milestones with Gabriel: potty training and growth spurts; his first Christmas and his first ever full sentence – 'I want to go home, I'm a bit tired.' He seemed happy, and as such more secure and confident; he knew he was here to stay. But it was difficult for him to understand where we'd come from. I remember one conversation, when he was almost three, when he said he'd bought us in a shop. He was also aware that he didn't look like us: he would describe his skin as brown, Harry's as white with blue bits, while mine was yellow. Our social worker Jacqui (Satwinder had by then left for a new job) said it was an unusual observation for someone so young.

Walking down the street with Harry one day he pointed to a black passerby and said, 'That's my brown Daddy.' 'If that's your brown Daddy, who am I?' Harry wanted to know. 'My silver Daddy,' he replied.

After nine months we met up with Bill and Mary again, this time on neutral territory at a butterfly farm, and again it was wonderful for Gabriel but painful for us. They were intimate and affectionate as they shared old rituals – Gabriel whispered in their ears and rubbed noses with them. Before we left, he sat on Bill's lap and felt his face with his hands. 'It's like watching your boyfriend meet up with an old lover and being witness to all the love that's still there,' I wrote in my diary.

Just before Gabriel's third birthday, we moved house. We hadn't anticipated the fallout, it hadn't occurred to us that he'd react so strongly, or miss what he called, 'The Old House' so much. He fell into another 'black hole', which is how we'd describe his bad moods, which could last a few weeks, or months with varying degrees of intensity.

Frequently he'd have three tantrums before 8am. His face would contort with rage; he'd open his mouth and scream up to an hour, sometimes in public. Anything could set him off: if I'd flushed the toilet when he wanted to; if he couldn't have rice pudding before dinner; he didn't want to put his socks on, finish watching *Fireman Sam*, or if I'd put the top on the toothpaste instead of him.

Of course it was all typical tyrant toddler behaviour, but I was more concerned about how it made me feel. I worried that the love I now felt would disappear. 'I don't have unconditional love,' I wrote with anger in my diary. 'It's totally conditional.' There were times when I shouted and the shame and guilt I felt afterwards was terrible. My anger wasn't always confined to home; I'd sunk so low, I even had a row with my yoga teacher. The childcare books told you to stay calm, be consistent and forgive. But I'd sulk. 'Are you talking to me, Mummy?' Gabriel would ask. I couldn't understand why life with him seemed to be getting more difficult, rather than easier. Surely the longer he was with us, the more secure he should feel? Talking to other mothers gave me some reassurance: one mother confessed she sometimes wanted to slap her child – she never did, but the desire was there; another said she sometimes plotted against hers. I wanted to run away. And I did for a few days – I went to New York to visit my sister, who was working there, and then felt like a bad mother when I didn't want to come home. I lived in fear of Gabriel's moods: what if he refused to get dressed in the morning and made me late for work? What if he refused to go to nursery? What if he never stopped having tantrums? What if he had severe behavioural problems that we hadn't been told about? Both Harry and my mother, the two other adults who loved him and spent the most time with him, refused to share my catastrophic thoughts. He's a lovely boy, they told me. He's just not behaving himself at the moment.

It was around this time that Gabriel also rejected Harry. He'd gone through phases before when he'd cling to me more, which I quite enjoyed – it made me feel important, special. But this was different; it felt like a sustained attack on the pair of us. He refused to allow Harry to dress, feed or bathe him, put him to bed or get him up in the morning, or comfort him if he woke in the night. A stickler for detail, he'd scream if Harry did things in a different way to me. He'd deliberately drop things on the floor for him to pick up, or would complain if he pushed the buggy the wrong way. His favourite words became, 'I want', 'I need' or simply 'No'.

'I felt like I was a rubbish dad, and questioned everything I did,' says Harry now. 'I just took the blame and assumed I was doing everything wrong.' His confidence was undermined and my patience was running out. Gabriel became dependent on me for everything – even walking, which he'd often refuse to do up and down stairs. His demands were relentless. I could feel none of the positives of fulfilling another's needs – the warmth, the sense of purpose, the kindness – I just felt at the beck and call of a tyrant.

We'd talk about it endlessly and felt relieved when he was asleep. When Harry needed a break, I'd send him down the pub with a newspaper. Maybe it was because we talked about nothing else that we were able to work through it and not turn on each other. I remember hearing a theory that it was common for boys of Gabriel's age, around three-and-a-half, to fall in love with their mothers. But that didn't help; I wasn't able to please him any more than Harry was.

During one particularly impressive screaming fit, while I was attempting to bathe him, I remember shaking with anger, my face drained of any colour. Five minutes later, when I popped into his bedroom to say goodnight, he said, 'I love you, Mummy.' It was the first time he'd ever said it, unprompted, and all my stress and tension evaporated.

For all his controlling, tyrannical moods, Gabriel was growing into a lively, imaginative, loving, funny, sociable child. I'd hear him muttering in his bedroom as he played, putting 'food' in a hat for his toy horse, or running away from monsters and bears. He developed stock phrases: 'I didn't mean to do it on purpose' or 'That's your pleasure, that's your welcome'. When I once asked him how much toy money he had, he said, 'Half past two pounds.'

His mood eventually lifted and the reign of tyranny, which in its most intense phase had lasted a couple of months, ended. He and Harry were friends again. After 15 months, our Adoption Order was granted and we became his legal parents. We tried to rise to the occasion but it was difficult in the grey surroundings of the local county court, where we had the final hearing. We were given a 'celebration certificate' (the official documents would be sent later), which we all signed, including the Judge and Gabriel with a scrawl, and then went off for a trip on the London Eye. It wasn't a success: halfway round, Gabriel wanted to get off, and was inconsolable by the time he was back on safe ground and in his buggy. He fell into an exhausted sleep while we celebrated over a glass of warm wine in Pizza Express.

Finally, Gabriel was ours. We could take him out of the country without asking permission first, and he could take our surname; we no longer had to report to social workers, or prove ourselves as parents.

They couldn't take him away from us.

* * *

Gabriel had been with us for two years when we decided to have a Naming Ceremony – a humanist, non-religious Christening service. We saw it as an opportunity to officially welcome our son into the family and celebrate him in a way that we weren't able to when he first arrived for fear of overwhelming him.

About 60 of our family and friends, including both sets of grandparents, Gabriel's two aunts and his cousins, crammed into our small garden on a beautifully sunny summer afternoon two days after Gabriel's fourth birthday. We asked Sunita and her husband Chris to be Gabriel's 'guiding adults' or godparents, and a wonderfully calm, elderly and bearded officiant, Dennis, presided over the ceremony. He read out the words that Harry and I had written, describing our journey and thanking everyone who had helped us along the way. He was only four but Gabriel stood stock-still next to us, seeming to take it all in and recognising the significance. It felt like a wedding and everyone cried.

Harry was too emotional to give the speech he'd planned to make but luckily Gabriel's guiding adult, Chris, held it together to read his. 'We promise throughout the lifelong friendship that we have embarked on with him that we will never be distant,' he told everyone. 'We will be ever present to listen to him, to encourage him, to help him make the tough decisions, to pick him up and dust him off. And to explain, probably around the age of 15, that his parents really do have his best interests at heart. And of course to tell him that we love him, but also that we admire him, as I'm pretty sure, all of us here already do.'

* * *

I once asked my mum to write down her memories of those first few months and years. It's easy to overlook the impact an adoption has on wider family and friends.

'I was really impressed at how capable you both were – although that mightn't have been how you were both feeling,' she wrote. 'You were so positive and determined to get it right, and were clear as to how you wanted things to go – that is, I wasn't allowed to visit until he had settled in as you wanted to do things by the book.

'I was apprehensive when I was finally invited to meet him, but I can honestly say within minutes I fell in love. He was such a friendly, smiley child and irresistible. I was so relieved I liked him so much, I was dreading perhaps not being able to bond with this unknown child, but there was never any problem and I loved him from the start. He wasn't reserved or shy, and easy to like.

'I know you warned me not to get too starry-eyed about my memories, but I have felt blessed that Gabriel is my grandson.'

Chapter Eight

Rebecca has been punched, bitten, kicked, spat at and verbally abused by her two adopted daughters. Her eldest, Alice, once gave her two black eyes.

'I was telling her off about something and touched her on the shoulder. She turned round and whacked me full force in the face. It was instinctive. And she looked terrified.'

People tell her she's a saint for having adopted her girls. She says, 'I'm just trying to be a mum.'

This is parenting on a completely different scale to the one we've been used to. Maybe at times I've underestimated our roles as adoptive parents. It's had its challenges but nothing to the degree faced by those who have taken on the children we didn't feel capable of parenting – the ones who have been strapped in a baby seat for hours, left in a room, locked outside, hit or abused, not fed, clothed or loved in any way.

As much as I wanted to write this book to share a

positive story of adoption, I'm aware that our experience won't reflect everybody's. Many adopters have struggled with situations I'm not sure I could have coped with. I wanted to explore some of them in this chapter.

In various workshops we'd learnt a bit about the long-term impact of emotional and physical abuse and neglect on children; how if a child felt repeatedly abandoned, isolated, or uncared for, they would have problems in attaching or forming secure relationships. There is also now a growing understanding of the impact of life experiences on the neurological, as well as psychological, development in children, particularly babies.

'A lot of the children we work with find it terribly hard to settle and concentrate because they've had to be vigilant,' explains Jeanne Kaniuk, managing director of Coram's adoption services. 'They've learnt from being tiny that you have to keep an eye on the environment and monitor what's going on. It makes it very hard to settle, and a lot of these children have difficulty in being able to calm themselves.'

'If a baby is properly looked after,' explains Alan Burnell, co-director of Family Futures, an adoption and adoption support agency, 'then it learns to trust the mother and the environment, and sees it as good. If none of that happens, then the baby is distressed and operates on a very primitive brain level – it goes into flight, fight or freeze mode, because it feels threatened.

'If the baby cries out and nothing happens, then it shuts down, and goes into despair – and despair for a baby is a physiological feeling of impending doom.'

I tell Burnell that it makes me feel incredibly sad.

'And that's only half of it,' he tells me. 'It's the horrible cocktail of neglect, abuse and maltreatment. If a child's experience of the world is scary, for whatever reason, then the brain will be more wired up for fear responses than a baby that's had a very positive, secure and non-threatening experience.'

On an emotional level, a child will find it difficult to love or trust an adult unless they've experienced that love and trust for themselves. 'If your experience of being with a parent is basically scary, you develop strategies for coping, which are either to become avoidant and invisible because you fear you might get shouted at or hurt, or to become very demanding and attention seeking, or to become aggressive and self-reliant,' explains Burnell, whose organisation helps up to 60 families, offering therapy and counselling to both adoptive parents and children. 'Some children have all three at different stages or times.'

He set up Family Futures 18 years ago when it became clear that increasing numbers of parents taking on older children were experiencing more difficulties than those who had adopted babies.

'We feel strongly that it's immoral to place children with complex needs with people who have never parented before and leave them to get on with it,' he explains.

According to Julie Selwyn, professor of child and family social work at the University of Bristol, there is an 'anti lobby' of those who believe that such damaged children are not so easily rehabilitated.

'There's one group of academics who are arguing about the long-term impact of abuse and neglect, saying that you really have to recognise that sometimes permanent damage is done to children and that there are real difficulties. Then there's another lobby that says that's too deterministic, and that social work is all about change; that we shouldn't be talking like this, it's too medicalised. Attacks go backwards and forwards – it's so political.'

Meanwhile the adoptive parents who do take on these kids are 'extraordinary,' says Alan Burnell. 'I'm always awestruck at how robust they are.'

When I was researching this chapter what struck me most about the people I spoke to were their common characteristics – optimism, resilience and a sense of humour – all of which have carried them through the hard times.

In fact, I'm amazed at just how upbeat Rebecca, 56, is. Smartly dressed in a Jaeger coat and brogues, she laughs easily, often at the disturbing behaviour she's had to deal with, on her own, with her daughters, Alice, 16, and 11-year-old Phoebe.

I look for signs of anxiety in her face, but I can't see any. Nor does she express any self-pity. Her apparent calmness in the face of the storm, she says, is down to the support she's received from Family Futures – the whole family has therapy there. Her therapist is just a supportive text message away. Even so, it takes more than therapy to deal with some of the daily challenges with such apparent buoyancy.

'I've always been an optimist, and very positive,' she explains, as we try to talk quietly in a busy café. 'If I see a problem, I want to solve it. I'm good in a crisis. I wouldn't describe myself as very patient but I've changed my attitude at how I look at my daughters, and have been able to detach myself a bit. So when they're calling me all the names under the sun – Alice not so much, but Phoebe does – I'm thinking, "This isn't her calling me these things, it's her fear." But it's taken a huge amount of time for me to reach that mindset.'

A former physiotherapist who now works part-time as a patient safety manager at a hospital, Rebecca, who is single, decided to adopt when she was 40. Her last serious relationship had ended in her early 30s and although she considered having a child through IVF and sperm donation, she didn't go through with it. After deciding to adopt she was taken on by a local authority and, rather naïvely she thinks now, was approved to adopt two siblings between the ages of two and eight. 'I thought if I was prepared to take two siblings, I would stand a better chance of getting children,' she says. She was prepared to consider children with mild learning disabilities or a physical disability, but wanted them to be able to maintain their own independence and, 'go on to lead active, fulfilling lives'.

Alice and Phoebe were placed with her in July 2007, aged three and nine. The sisters had been in foster care for 18 months before that. In retrospect, she wishes she'd asked more questions. 'There was so much onus on me to say what I wanted to know, but the social workers didn't seem to be able to use their professional experience to guide me. They kept saying, "You need to decide what questions to ask." Or they'd say, "It's going to be really hard," and I'd think, "But I don't know *how* hard. I've never been a parent before, so how can I know?"'

When Rebecca was shown details of her daughters they 'jumped out' at her – 'They looked so sweet.' She was told that they'd come from a chaotic family situation and suffered neglect. There was a hint of domestic violence but no mention of their birth mother having taken drugs or alcohol – although Rebecca has since discovered that she probably did. It's also likely that the girls had been sexually abused. She was told that Alice was 'a little behind at school' when in fact she had a significant learning difficulty and ADHD, and has needed to go to a special school.

Rebecca says the cynical side of her believes that the girls' social workers were economical with the truth for fear they wouldn't be placed. But, desperate to be a mum, she also acknowledges that there may have been some denial on her part.

She harboured a fantasy of what life would be like when the children moved in. 'We'd go on lovely walks, and holidays, mooch around the shops, do a bit of cooking together. Christmas would be gingerbread houses.' The reality, which she discovered just weeks after they'd come to live with her in July 2007, was very different.

'Alice would come home from school completely dysregulated. She would turn into a violent whirlwind, fighting, kicking and hitting. Sometimes she'd hit out on impulse, almost as a survival instinct. But most of the time it was challenging – "I want to fight against you because I don't trust you – how can I? You're just another adult."'

'She used to be full of remorse afterwards, which was very draining as I'd think, "Look, you've done it now, you've said sorry." But she didn't have any control and was terrified of being sent away.'

Both girls received help from CAMHS (Child and Adolescence Mental Health Service), and Alice was medicated for ADHD. After a couple of years, the violence slowly ceased. She can now talk about what happened in her past, and has strong memories of her birth family. 'In her limited intelligence she can say, "That's bad, that shouldn't have happened to me," but spends a lot of time blaming herself although she is coming round to the fact that it's not her fault.'

Alice has also formed an attachment to Rebecca, whereas Phoebe hasn't. In public, Rebecca says, Phoebe is a polite, charming, smiley girl, who is well behaved at school, with a normal IQ. At home, however, she is hostile, aggressive and fearful – she won't go upstairs or to the bathroom on her own, has nightmares every night and two years ago became violent, like her sister before her. 'She bites and pinches, spits and swears, and will say anything to try and revolt me, because she's full of repulsion for herself,' explains Rebecca, fiddling with the loom band ring on her finger that her youngest daughter made for her. Phoebe now sees a psychiatrist at Family Futures; she has been diagnosed with extreme anxiety as well as being hyper-vigilant.

It is at this point I ask Rebecca how she has coped – how she can sit and hold a normal conversation with me. 'Well, you have to, don't you?' she says. 'But there are days when I've burst into tears.' She is also on anti-depressants. Support from Family Futures, who she started seeing for therapy for both herself and the girls two years ago after fighting for funding, has proved a lifesaver, especially a year ago, when she came close to giving up – 'They said to me, "You're doing an amazing job." And in my moments, I can see that I am making a difference.'

Alice, she says, has, 'developed into a beautiful,

responsive child. She has lots of friends, and is involved in clubs for kids with learning difficulties. She can't do many things on her own – she's too scared of the outside world, and too vulnerable. But she's really allowing me to be her mum, and that's lovely.

'She can be funny, and a right old pain in the a*** sometimes because she's a teenager, but it's reassuring that she can be naughty and argue about things.'

For now, Rebecca can't see Phoebe ever accepting her as her mother.

'I'm a supporter, a carer who will fight her cause, and she will rely on me for basics – clothes, food, heating. But she can't allow me to love her.

'Even if I have to think of it like a job to educate her and keep her out of prison, then that's fine. If she never loves me, never attaches to me, and has horrendous issues, then at least she will be well educated and be someone, perhaps, who contributes to society.'

For Alice she sees a brighter future – maybe leading a semi-independent life at a residential college. 'But I can't see into the future for Phoebe. I fear for her in relationship terms. She's always said, "I'm never going to leave home, I'm always going to live here," and I'm like, great!' she laughs. 'There I'll be in my Stannah stairlift, thinking, "All I want is a gin."'

What about her own future? Does she ever allow herself to think about her own needs? 'It would be lovely to have a man, but a relationship would have to make my life better, and at the moment it can't. It would have to be someone so understanding.'

So, for now, she remains on her own, deeply committed

to raising her two girls. What, I wonder, has she got from it?

'I have a need to be needed, so they satisfy that. There are two people who rely on me completely and utterly, and will actually do nice things for me. We can do nice things together, and I've met lots of different people through it.

'I have given them a life, and I still am. I can't give up on them.'

* * *

Barbara, a social worker, and Jeff, a civil servant, both 47, had been together for 'years' before they began to think about starting a family – 'We were happily living in London, going out dancing, getting wrecked. It was fab!'

After discovering that they couldn't have children naturally without fertility treatment, they went through three 'awful, terrible' rounds of IVF, one of which resulted in an ectopic pregnancy. In 2004, they decided to look at adoption. 'There was the intellectual, social worker side of me then there was the "Shit, what are we doing?"' Barbara explains, 'And the side of me that wanted to be a parent.'

As a social worker specialising in adoption who helps place children with families she has a deep understanding and knowledge of the issues involved but her drive to adopt was purely maternal.

'I was looking at it from a perspective of a woman who was desperate to be a mother, rather than thinking of it from a social worker's point of view,' she explains. '[My job] gave me a lot of insight into what to expect. It also made the process easier because I understood it. But I was still going through it as me, as someone who hadn't looked after children in her home.'

Their two sibling daughters, Shannon, 14, and Emma, 12, came to live with them eight and a half years ago. Asked to describe them, she says it depends on what day it is. 'The older one is fun, active, loyal to her friends, lively, energetic and funny. The younger one is sensitive, creative, charming and tries her best.'

Both, however, have struggled with their difficult backgrounds.

'They'd suffered chronic neglect, physical abuse, inappropriate behaviour in and out of the house, multiple moves. The parents had split up before the youngest was born so there were lots of separations, including from each other,' Barbara continues. 'They'd been left with people who wouldn't have had their interests on their list of priorities.'

Despite this background of 'scary chaos' the girls had shown no serious behavioural issues, were happy, playful and had a good relationship with each other. 'There was nothing very worrying about their behaviour, nothing that I wasn't expecting.' When they first came to live with their new parents, however, they didn't know how to play.

'They'd never learnt,' says Barbara, 'so when other children came over they didn't know what to do.' They could kick a ball outside, or climb a tree, but when it came to imaginative play, like schools or with made-up figures, 'they didn't have a clue, or understand why you'd want to do it in the first place. My eldest would build spectacular things out of Lego, and then that would be it – it wouldn't occur to her to play with it.'

Perhaps it's the calm and considered way in which she talks – she thinks carefully about my questions before answering them – but there is something authoritative and reassuring about Barbara. She seems unflappable, and expresses a deep understanding and acceptance of her daughters. Both have struggled – Shannon has been angry and grieved for her birth family at different points throughout her childhood, Emma has had periods of self-harming.

'There's been lying, stealing and swearing, and not doing homework and stuff that I think is normal – although my husband doesn't,' says Barbara. 'Deception and food hoarding and appalling hygiene, stuff that comes from feeling really bad about yourself – I don't think I'd label that as behavioural difficulties. I know to expect that kind of stuff and manage it, whereas other parents might be more challenged by it.'

She's been accepting – if not stoic – when her eldest daughter has rejected her.

'She's said to me lots of times, "You're not my mother." The other day she said, "You're more like a care worker, aren't you?" But it doesn't make me feel as bad as other people think it should. I understood why she said it – I understood that she felt so awful about herself that she couldn't let me get close to her. She wanted me to reject her.

'One of the hard things for me is keeping things in,' she admits. 'A lot of friends have said things to their children in anger, and felt bad about it. But if I said some of the things that were inside me in anger, it would be extremely damaging so I have to stay one step ahead in terms of reining myself in.'

Rebecca told me that her daughters needed 'exceptional parenting' and Barbara agrees. Both try to parent in what they call a 'therapeutic' way – that is, without punishment. I can't imagine the patience it requires, the self-discipline it must take not to fight back, but apparently it works.

'We don't discipline in a punitive way, but by keeping them close and using empathy. We praise more than criticise. It's about consistency and fairness and being a good role model, and not rejecting them or sending them away if they've done something I don't like, as that can make them feel even more angry, rejected and alone. I believe it works and that's why we've got a close relationship with both of them,' Barbara explains.

'But I surround myself with people who get it,' she adds. 'I think it must be very isolating for people who are trying to parent their children therapeutically when around others who don't understand, and who say, "I don't know why you don't just tell them off."'

'I understand it, but it's still hard,' admits Rebecca, who also tries to practice therapeutic parenting. 'It goes against the grain of my upbringing, in terms of there being no consequences [for bad behaviour]. They can be shouting at you, or calling you names, and you don't say, "Go to your room," you have to say, "Oh, I love you." But I can see it working. And when I used to try and make them sit on a naughty step they didn't really understand why they were sitting there.'

What's helped Barbara to go 'Bleurgh' – as she calls it – has been lots of psychotherapy and support groups, some of which she helps run. Her husband, she admits, has struggled more than her. 'I knew what to expect more than he did. I think I'm very resilient and when things have been bad, I still wake up and feel optimistic about the day. Even when things have been dire, I've kept going. He has found it much harder. I try to be calm and floaty, he's a bit more noisy.'

I think it's the level of empathy that Barbara feels for her children that lies at the heart of her ability to parent them. She concedes, 'Adoption has been the best thing for our children,' but also believes, 'It's crap being adopted. It makes you feel different. And all these changes are made to your life without [you] being consulted. You have no choice about your family, no right to reply; no escape route. I'm living with two children who are extremely damaged by their experiences so if I asked them, "Are you glad you were adopted?" they'd both say no. There's an underlying feeling that what's happened to them is really unfair and horrible.'

But they now have her and Jeff, I say.

'Yes, of course, but for them living their lives, it's still unfair.'

This is where, I think, the boundaries between her personal and professional life become blurred. 'Because I'm a social worker and an adopter, I'm working and living it, so it's hard for me sometimes to know what point of view I'm coming from,' she admits.

I think her daughters are lucky to have her.

* * *

Lila, seven, had been with them for just a few weeks when Helen broke down in Tesco. 'I called my social worker and said, "I can't do this," and the next day a couple of them came and sat with me for three hours, and listened,' she remembers. 'They tried to explain to me why Lila was behaving the way she was – that everything was new to her, she was scared, and that some of what she was doing was a good sign. I always think it's weird when they say, "If they're lovely outside but turn when they're at home it's a sign they're relaxed." I was like, "Great, thanks".'

Helen, 46, a complementary therapist, and her husband Martin, 51, who works in engineering, had adopted Lila when she was five years old, having tried and failed to have children naturally. They hadn't particularly been looking at older children, but a picture of Lila took their breath away, says Helen, because of their close physical resemblance. The pair went into it fully informed and with their eyes wide open – Lila had lived with her birth mother, who suffered mental health issues, and her home life was chaotic and volatile. They were told that she suffered from high anxiety, low self-esteem and mood swings, and had some attachment issues. She'd had two foster placements after being removed from her birth mum at three years old.

'We weren't in it to adopt a healthy baby who'd suffered no trauma, as we knew that wouldn't be the case,' explains Helen. 'Martin and I have had our fair share of emotional upsets and we've got through it. Also, being a complementary therapist, I've studied stress and have helped people with it, so I thought I understood maybe more than others. I thought we could deal with it.'

But the reality, she discovered, was quite different. A few weeks after Lila's arrival Martin went back to work, Lila went back to school and Helen became depressed. She describes the first few months as 'awful'.

'It was like walking on eggshells. Lila wouldn't talk to me after school, and if I asked, she'd say, "Why do I have to tell you?" She'd demand food, then she'd start screaming. She'd hate it if I sat next to her, so I'd get the ironing out to be near her, and she'd say, "Why do you have to be in the same room as me?" But if I went somewhere else she'd want to know where I was and follow me around. She was very controlling. She'd hate it when Martin came home, and would say, "I don't like Daddy." For the first six months we had to keep telling her, "We do things as a family – it's the three of us."'

'In those first few months,' says Helen, 'I felt a failure. I felt as if I'd lost my freedom and my confidence. I'd disappeared.' In retrospect, she thinks she suffered post-adoption depression. Luckily, she has received plenty of support, in particular ten two-hourly counselling sessions over Skype with an experienced counsellor and social worker who has given advice and strategies, and helped the couple understand their daughter's behaviour.

'In the very early days we thought, "We can't do this – it's a wrong match." But then we could see why they'd matched us for her sake: it wasn't about us, it was about Lila. We're a very stable, secure and quiet house, we're really quite boring, and that's what she needed, this calmness. And they [the social workers] did everything they could to help us.'

She has also sought solace from the adoption community on social media – using Twitter, reading blogs and getting advice.

'If you've had a shitty day you can go onto Twitter and you get people asking if you're OK, which is lovely. Also, when I hear about other adopters I think, "Why am I moaning?" OK, Lila has anxiety and needs to be treated differently – she doesn't have the same resilience that other children have, or the same understanding about life – but I can often think, "We've got it OK, actually".'

Helen believes that potential adopters need to be more prepared for what might lie ahead – even at the risk of putting them off. 'More needs to be done in terms of painting a worse-case scenario,' she says. 'It can be balanced with good stories, but they've got to show that these kids are going to suffer from trauma.'

For those working in the field, balancing the need to prepare potential adopters while encouraging them to come forward is a difficult one. Children don't fit neatly into categories or always conform to prescribed patterns of behaviour: some have the ability to cope better than others.

'The trouble is, even with little children, it's very difficult to predict which one will do swimmingly well once they've found a loving family. With some of them, even if they're adopted very young, the difficulties persist,' explains Coram's Jeanne Kaniuk. 'Some children are more vulnerable, are born with less resilience. Some of them have had more of a rough time than we know. Sometimes the chemistry works, for others it's not quite as good a fit.

'But people have to understand what they're getting into because it's a big deal: parenting's a big deal. Once you're responsible for these little people, they're in your heart forever.'

Two years on, and life is a lot calmer for Helen and Martin, who no longer feel they're treading on eggshells. They know how to manage Lila's mood swings and what may trigger them. 'We have a really good life. A lot of things that the social worker said we wouldn't be able to do, we have done. Martin and I love travelling, and we can do that with her, no problem. She loves going out and about. I love her, she's an adorable, delightful child – most of the time,' Helen smiles. 'I wouldn't be without her.'

* * *

'For us the whole experience has been like having a broken piece of very delicate china that you have to put back together, one piece at a time,' wrote Dawn, 41, in an email to me about adopting her son Billy, now nine. 'Sometimes you get a piece wrong and have to start again.'

I warmed to her as soon as I read her description, which she'd sent in response to a request I'd put out to speak to adopters. When we eventually spoke, I liked her even more. Not only for the way in which she talks about her son, whom she describes as, 'loving, unpredictable, happy and eager to please,' but also because her family demonstrates the transformative effect that adoption can have on an older child's life.

While negative early-life experiences such as abuse and neglect can damage us, a secure, nurturing environment can also repair us, explains Family Futures' Alan Burnell. The brain's 'plasticity' enables it to change and re-organise with high-quality parenting and therapeutic input.

'As a rule of thumb, the longer a child has been in an abusive environment, the harder it is for them to be re-parented,' he explains, 'although not impossible. The very thing that makes us vulnerable to poor parenting is the very thing that makes us receptive to good parenting. If the child begins to have more good experiences, then that will change the way they perceive the world.'

'Over time, children who come from really complicated backgrounds can develop a much more positive attachment, and therefore more hopeful expectation of the world,' says Coram's Jeanne Kaniuk.

There is also that element in any successful adoption – fate or chemistry, synchronicity or serendipity – that cannot be assessed or monitored. It's what some of the experts call 'narcissistic identification'. 'There has to be something in the child that resonates with you,' says Burnell. 'In biological children, it's easier because they often look like you, so you can think, "It's a little me." But for children who are coming into adoptive families, it's helpful if an adoptive parent can think, "I don't know what it is about this kid but there's something about them..." It might be something about the child's history that resonates, it might be the way they look, it could even be something as primitive as smell.'

As Jeanne Kaniuk says, 'It's a jolly mysterious process.'

'The bottom line is that we can't predict which kids are going to create tremendous difficulties, and which aren't,' says Julie Selwyn, Professor of child and family social work at the University of Bristol. 'We can say which children are carrying which risks, but you can't predict. In the States, they adopt many teenagers, because they find families who are willing to give it a go. It's not always about the age. Imagine writing off a six-year-old, just because they're six,' she says, 'I find that really tough.'

For Dawn, a nanny, and her husband, Stuey, who works for a furniture factory, the synchronicity happened as soon as a piece of paper was slid across the table to them in their social worker's office. 'That was it, there was no other child,' says Dawn. 'It was just going to be him.'

The fact that Billy was half-Welsh, like Stuey, and looked a lot like him too, was a contributing factor. 'But everyone says, "You know when it's the right child," and he just felt like the right child for us.'

That was despite the fact that, at eight years old, he was older than they'd been prepared to consider (which had been a child no more than five). They made the decision to adopt ten years after going through 'disastrous' IVF treatment and knew they weren't interested in very young children – Dawn had looked after lots of babies in her job and her husband wanted someone to play with. 'We talked and read about it a lot, and realised that any problems were probably going to be more obvious [in older children], whereas with babies, you assume they're "normal" but then things can come out later.'

They were shown Billy's details a couple of weeks before they were approved. He came from a big sibling group, his birth parents had a serious drug issue and he was removed from the family home, where he'd witnessed a lot of domestic violence, at four-and-a-half, when he first went to live with a maternal aunt for a year, and then went into foster care. Just before his eighth birthday he came to Dawn and Stuey.

'We were told he was emotionally immature, as you'd expect. He would have a paddy like a three-year-old, and when I say "paddy", he would lay on the floor and flail around if you said no to something,' remembers Dawn.

As time has gone by, they've learned more from Billy about what his life was like with his birth family.

'He has told us that if he cried, they'd lock him in a cupboard. They used to lock the kids outside for hours on end.

I discovered this when I was out with him one day, and the door banged shut behind us and Billy freaked out, saying, "Daddy's locked us out, Daddy's locked us out!"

'He doesn't like to go upstairs when it's dark, and that's because quite often they'd go upstairs and people would be taking drugs in the bedrooms. He's seen both parents arrested on numerous occasions, and when the police came to the house, they'd hide under the bed. He's only got to see the police around somewhere and he's really worried. He's asked a lot about drugs and why people take them, and it's difficult to explain. He's paranoid about going to prison and I have to reassure him, "But you're not going to go."'

These must be difficult things to hear, as his mum. 'They are hard,' she agrees, 'and Stuey gets very angry about it. He's our child now and to think that anyone did that to him is horrible. But we say to him, "It's never going to happen again, no one is going to hit or hurt you," but building up that trust was hard to start with. He would push and push us, almost as if he wanted a reaction. He's punched and kicked Stuey, trying everything to get him to retaliate. But he's got a lot better about that now and will say, "No one's going to hurt me."'

She believes in many ways Billy was lucky in that he had older siblings who would protect and look after him – in particular, an older brother who parented him and with whom Billy meets up at least twice a year. That bonding relationship has enabled him to form attachments with others. But it's not happened overnight and there have been times, especially in the early days, when all three of them struggled.

'When we first had him he used to really struggle to sleep, and I thought, "What do I do?" I'd read that rocking children and regressing them, like a baby, could really help. So I wrapped him in a blanket a few times, and sat with him, which he really liked. He also has very vivid nightmares about things that have happened so often he'll get into our bed on one side and one of us gets out of bed on the other!

'One night, I sat with him while he cried until 4am. I said to him, "Why are you crying?" and he said, "I don't know, Mummy. I don't know." But I think he was probably emotionally relieved that he had stability; that he was going to stay. I think a lot of love, consistency and feeling safe has been massive for him. He lived on his nerves before. He came here and was able to relax.'

There have been times when she has sat down and cried – often because of something Billy has told her about his past. They've had their battles, which she has tried to diffuse with humour. 'If he's being a bit stroppy, we'll just laugh at him and that tends to pull him around.' And despite the concerns of friends and family – 'When I first told my mum she said, "Why are you having a child that age? Don't you want a baby?"' – adopting an eight-year-old has been much easier than she anticipated.

'I think I've watched too much *Tracy Beaker*,' she jokes, 'but we were expecting a child to arrive and not want to be with us. Actually he's always wanted to be here, and he's always been responsive.'

He is, she tells me proudly, 'very lovable'. 'He has an endearing personality and has people eating out of his hand. He can't do any wrong for one set of godparents. They'll say, "He's gorgeous."'

Maybe they have been lucky with Billy, but Dawn believes given the chance, children will, 'blossom and flourish'. She strongly believes that older children in particular need to be given the chance of adoption.

'They get too much bad press – that they come into your home, steal your money, wreck your house and then walk away. Everyone assumes it's going to be a disaster, but it's not.

'We always said that [adopting Billy] was an amazing risk, like jumping off a cliff, and we could have hit the floor. But we haven't,' she says. It's something she likes to stress when she talks to potential adopters as part of the voluntary work she now does for her adoption agency.

'They're like, "But they're never going to function on a normal level," and I say, "Well, I have a nine-year-old who hurls himself around a rugby field every Sunday, who has friends round for tea, goes for sleepovers. We take him away left, right and centre, and he doesn't bat an eyelid, goes to school quite happily, has never got into trouble, tries really hard and is happy 99 per cent of the time." And they look at me and go, "Really? What have you done to him?" And I say, "Given him a lot of love and a lot of time."'

Is love enough for these kids?

'Maybe it's not, maybe we were just lucky, but he was just the right child for us, and we were the right people for him.'

Chapter Nine

Small boys are strange creatures and Gabriel is no exception. He never walks but jumps down the stairs, rolls on floors and bounces on beds with loud 'Oouffs'. He loves Michael Jackson, wearing *Star Wars* pants and collecting obsessively – first Ben 10s, then Gogos, now Match Attax and Beyblades. He prefers not to practise piano, walk to school, tie his own laces or butter his own toast. He puts signs on his door saying, 'Do Not Disturb, Gabriel is inventing something', and passes me notes scrawled with, 'I love you' or 'Can I watch TV?' He makes sudden, unexpected appearances dressed as a Ninja, vampire or King Arthur and puts our dog in goal as Gordon Banks when he plays football in the garden. He'd like to be in the Guinness World Records for having the longest big toenail in the world and wishes wobbly teeth had never been invented.

He can frustrate and annoy me, worry and concern me, but no more so, I believe, than any other nine-year-old does any other parent. To all intents and purposes we are a 'normal' family and Gabriel is completely 'our' son – although, in another sense, we're not, and he isn't.

He was three-and-a-half years old when we first told him a simplified version of his adoption story, which has formed the backbone ever since: That he was a beautiful baby; that his birth mother loved him but couldn't look after him; that Bill and Mary looked after him and loved him until his mummy and daddy could be found. And here we are now, together, forever. Bit by bit, details of the story will be added, as and when he is ready to hear them. In the meantime we continue to get on with our lives. I so rarely think of him as being adopted that it can come as a surprise if I'm reminded of it.

But every so often I'll come across an assumption about adoption that annoys me. An American author and academic, Ken Watson, once wrote in *Meeting the Challenge of Successful Adoptive Parenting: A New Way of Looking at Adoption* that adoption practice has been developed on a set of principles that 'can now be recognized as *myths*' (his italics). He describes one such myth as: 'An adoptive child can as fully belong to an adoptive family as a child born to that family.' He also writes that, 'Adoption complicates the lives of those involved throughout their lives.' Call me possessive, but I can't imagine any birth child of mine any more belonging to my family than Gabriel already does. I also believe that *any* family complicates the lives of those involved, not just adoptive families.

And yet... while I don't subscribe to what I think are extreme views, I understand that as a family we must deal with challenges that are specific to adoption. We have to

178

help Gabriel understand where he has come from, why he couldn't stay there, and hope our love will paper over the cracks. We need to explain when friends or strangers ask awkward or nosey questions, or say insensitive things, or try to understand why his mood might swing if he feels insecure or threatened. We've attended workshops run by experts at our adoption agency to hear advice or share experiences with other adoptive parents. They're not compulsory, but designed to help with the parenting issues which are specific to adoption, such as how do you talk to your child about their past? And how does that past impact them at school? The need to attend these workshops recedes as your competence – and confidence – as an adoptive parent grows, but they were invaluable to begin with.

We need to tell Gabriel about the sadness and loss in his family history. I have to accept that, one day, he might feel abandoned and rejected, or fantasise about how his life might have been, even reject us. Or he might not. We may have to help him search for his birth family. Again, he might not want to look for them. But I do need to accept my sorrow that I didn't give birth to him, and that I'm not able to tell him about the day he was born.

* * *

As Gabriel approached school age we began thinking about where we'd like him to go. His nursery, which we loved, had a tiny prep school attached to it for children up to the age of seven. We knew if he went there it would be a seamless transition, as he'd start school with all his friends and be in the same building. But it would also cost us several thousand pounds a year.

We began to look at our local state schools as an alternative. Our main concern was that Gabriel should have security, stability and consistency. He was a well-adjusted, bright four-year-old but over the years he would begin to develop and have more of an understanding of his history and situation, and his difference to other children. As his sense of identity grew, so too, possibly, would his questions, and some insecurities. At a workshop on education issues for adopted parents we'd been told that as intellectual understanding in children developed around the ages of six, seven and eight, then so too did their understanding of adoption, which could bring with it some painful realisations. They could become distressed, angry or sad. Adopted children, as we'd experienced first-hand, didn't adjust well to change, so at certain times in the academic calendar, such as changing years and teachers, they could feel particularly vulnerable. All of the above might impact on a child's academic ability, which needed to be acknowledged, understood and dealt with sympathetically by the school. But above all else I felt – and still do – that Gabriel deserved every break in life he could get, including going to the best school. And I was prepared to fight for it.

We found a school in our local area that we both liked. It had an excellent reputation, both for its academic record and pastoral care, and a headmaster who understood our concerns – but it was incredibly over-subscribed. Still, we were confident that we'd get Gabriel in. I naively thought justice would prevail and that he'd get the school he deserved.

When we were applying for primary schools, children

in care, or 'looked after' children, were given priority by the local education authority and automatically granted a place at the school of their choice. It was ironic that our application went in just three months after we'd legally adopted Gabriel. Had we postponed the legalities, he would still be considered to be in 'Public Care' and made a priority. Obviously that hadn't occurred to us but still we felt we'd put forward a strong enough case.

A few weeks later we learnt we hadn't been offered a place. Furious at what I considered a huge injustice and primed for battle, we appealed. Armed with a passionate argument and a strong letter of support from our adoption agency, in June 2006 we faced a panel of educationalists in a grim civic centre for an appeal hearing, which we lost.

We've since felt vindicated. In 2012, the law changed in recognition of the anomaly between 'looked after' and adopted children, who are now given the same priority. We missed out on primary school but at least we wouldn't have to fight any battles for secondary school.

While all this was going on, I was dealing with an altogether different emotional battle – at the opposite end of the age spectrum. My elderly father, who lived alone, had been behaving in an increasingly erratic way. He wore layers of clothing – two pairs of trousers, several shirts, countless socks – as if he'd forgotten how many he'd put on. He didn't wash and had no concept of time. He forgot how to switch on a kettle, use his microwave or follow a conversation. Quite often he'd forget our names too. He had taken to carrying around a little pouch filled with cotton wool balls, his comb and some old boxing medals, and kept throwing large objects down the loo.

We managed to organise a bit of home help during the day but at night he became a danger to himself – emptying his cupboards of food and mixing ravioli with milk, coffee and soap powder, which he'd try to eat. Or he'd shave using deodorant rather than foam. My sister, my mother (from whom he'd been divorced for many years but remained friends with) and I kept up a daily rota of visits, terrified he might harm himself, or leave the house, wander off and become lost. It was exhausting.

Eventually he was admitted to the Elderly Mentally Ill ward of a psychiatric hospital for observation, where he was kept for three months, sharing a room with no windows and a curtain for a door, with other elderly men, some of them violent. He sat in an armchair all day, but retained moments of lucidity and a sharp sense of humour. When an orderly asked him what he would rather be called, Syd or Sydney, he quipped, 'Sir'. He was asked what he wanted to drink and he said, 'Champagne'. His wit cut through the madness. I'd visit him daily and when I left, he'd stand at the door (which was kept locked) and watch me through the window. When I came back the next day he'd still be standing there, wearing his coat and hat. 'Where have you been?' he'd ask me.

We were finally told, after three months, that he had both Alzheimer's and vascular dementia, and that he'd never be able to live in his own home again. After one particularly tough visit, a nurse reassured me that he was in the best place and that we, his family, could now take a rest from looking after him. She also told me to allow my emotions to run their course and prepare myself for the long haul, and to cherish those times when I could still talk to him because there would come a time when we wouldn't be able to have a conversation. She was right: inevitably, he eventually forgot who I was. He also forgot how to talk.

Along with the worry and guilt, sadness and exhaustion, I also felt resentment. It was summer, and I had planned to spend much of it with Gabriel, making the most of him before he started 'big' school in September 2006. But our outings to Richmond Park or the swimming pool were now punctuated by trips to the hospital, which unsettled Gabriel (especially the sporadic violent outbursts from other patients) or visits to nursing homes when it became clear that we had to find one for Dad to move into. This we had to do ourselves (the NHS service to help relatives had long been cut), putting his flat up for sale to pay for his long-term care.

My father's illness has nothing to do with adoption, of course, although an increasing number of people are finding that they, too, have to look after elderly parents while raising young children. I had become a member of what is now called the 'Sandwich Generation' (a generation of people, typically in their thirties or forties who care for their own children as well as their ageing parents). I noticed parallels between my father and son: as Gabriel grew less dependent and more capable of doing things for himself, my dad moved in the opposite direction. I'd gone from changing Gabriel's nappies to changing my dad's incontinence pads. Somehow their paths converged and grandfather and grandson reached a mutual understanding, based on talking nonsense. Both had an appreciation of the absurd, and enjoyed having incoherent conversations; they were on each other's level.

I have a picture of them both, my dad toothless (he kept losing his false teeth until one day they disappeared altogether) and wearing a Fez hat, with Gabriel standing next to him, his front teeth missing. They're looking at each other and laughing their heads off. Gabriel still can't talk about Grandad Syd (who died just under two years after his diagnosis) without becoming tearful.

In September, Gabriel started school and we moved my dad into a private nursing home. I'm grateful that Gabriel's first day of school wasn't as nerve-wracking as it might have been. We'd cut our losses and decided to send him to the tiny prep school attached to his nursery, so he started with the same friends in the same building. For a child resistant to change, it was perfect. I felt moved by the sight of him in his oversized uniform, the shorts hanging mid-calf and his big, black shiny shoes. It was a rite of passage deserving of a few tears, although I didn't expect to cry. He was safe and happy, but also a 'big' boy, with his own schedule, about which he could be frustratingly vague. His stock answer to any question about his school day was, 'Nothing' or 'Can't remember'. As a desperate measure, he'd resort to lying to get me off his back. Olivia had been sick all over the carpet and sent home (she hadn't). There'd been a fire and the building had collapsed (it hadn't). I later found out from his teachers that they were all at it – the kids were so small that their days stretched out interminably, so the question 'What did you do today?' was overwhelming. What *didn't* they do today?

Because the school was so small – there were only three years, with 20 kids in each year – it would have been hard to hide the fact that Gabriel was adopted, so I didn't even try. It was just over two years since he'd come home to us but it felt we were still finding our feet, not quite 'professional' parents yet. The playground was tiny and parents – predominantly the mums – would cluster in small groups. There was nowhere to hide. Everybody knew Gabriel was adopted, and we had to have faith in the fact that they would be sensible and sensitive to the information. Luckily, most of them were.

It was a year for milestones. A month after starting school, Gabriel stopped using a dummy. A month later, he rode his bike without stabilisers. At the end of the year, he played the lead role in the school's Christmas production, *The Bossy King*.

* * *

According to the experts, an adopted child's understanding of the adoption process goes through distinct phases as they develop and grow older. Up until the age of six, there's little differentiation between adoption and birth; they tend to equate them as the same thing. There's a big leap from the age of six when they begin to recognise the difference between being born into a family and being adopted, and need help in understanding the permanence of the adoptive family. From the age of eight, anxiety might start to creep in about the permanency of adoption – the adoptive family could potentially break down, or the birth parents might reclaim them in the future. They may also suffer what is called 'Adaptive Grieving', in that they begin to acknowledge the loss in adoption.

I've never been able to track or measure Gabriel's under-standing of his adoption quite so neatly. The adopted daughter of a friend has grilled her mum for answers since she could talk – Why am I adopted? Where do I come from? Who is my birth mother? But Gabriel, so far, hasn't.

'Do you have anything you want to ask me?'

'No.'

'Any feelings you want to talk about?'

'No.'

We've tried to act instinctively and take our lead from him. He's a naturally sunny child who likes to have fun – big discussions aren't his thing. When he does ask questions, or brings the subject up, it's usually in short bursts, when we least expect it, or when it's been prompted by other people. You can't always protect against the unkindness of strangers or even the tactlessness of friends.

Other people – especially children – could be phenomenally insensitive. Our first real experience of this threw our household into a state of emergency. Gabriel was six and had invited a school friend, Milo, over for a sleepover (his first ever). They'd had a great day: Harry had taken them to Battersea Park, I'd given them tea; they'd watched telly, had a bath and were now tucked up in bed; two clean, happy boys. An hour later we heard Gabriel wailing. We rushed upstairs to find him sitting, distraught, at the end of his bed.

'Milo says I've got two mummies…'

I felt my heart explode.

'And that Mummy isn't my real mummy,' he sobbed. 'But she *is!*'

Our home had been invaded and the carefully selected words with which Harry and I had built Gabriel's adoption story had been knocked down and trampled over. We'd never talked in terms of two mummies, but 'Birth Mother' and 'Mummy': there was a big difference. At that moment I wanted to throw Milo out into the night. Instead, I picked up Gabriel and carried him into our bedroom, where we sat in the armchair. I then explained, as gently as I could, that his birth mother grew him in her tummy but that I grew him in my heart, and that I was his 'real' mummy because I was the one who fed, washed and clothed him, read to him and loved him. Eventually he fell asleep. I then went in to deal with Milo, who was having none of it.

'But he doesn't understand,' he insisted.

'No, Milo, *you* don't understand,' I said.

We were on good terms with most of the parents at school. However, I couldn't tell them how to talk to their own children about Gabriel, I just had to hope they would do so in an informed and intelligent way. But that night I regretted having been so open.

A few months later, Gabriel temporarily disappeared into one of his 'black holes', prompted, we think, by change. Having put our names on the waiting list when we failed to get in the first time around, we had finally got him a place at the local state school. The prep school only went up to Year Two, and we knew we couldn't afford to keep him in private education, so we snapped up the school place. We'd been spoilt. At his prep school the class sizes had been so small he'd often received one-to-one attention in a nurturing environment. Many of his friends had been with him at nursery so there was continuity in his care and relationships. The offer from the state school came halfway through the first term in Year Two. He would not only be the 'new' boy, but the *late* new boy. It was a wrench for all of us when he left; he didn't want to leave his friends and make new ones, and I didn't want to have to face the terror of a whole new community of mothers in the playground – a substantially bigger one at that. Also, I wasn't quite sure how to deal with the question of Gabriel's adoption. We'd talked to the headmaster about it and were satisfied that the school was equipped to deal with any issues, should they arise – but should we make it common knowledge? We decided not to. I asked the one parent I already knew at the new school not to make it public.

'I didn't know it was a secret,' she said, reasonably enough.

'It's not a secret,' I told her. 'It's just private and I don't want Gabriel to be defined by his background. And I want him to tell friends only when he wants to.'

Although he was going into a bigger, and possibly less intimate environment, I realised it would be more difficult to control information but Gabriel seemed to settle in quickly and made new friends easily.

At Christmas we went on holiday to Australia for a month following a bizarre stroke of good fortune. Years earlier, Harry and I had gone to a raffle at an art studio where, for £30, guests were given a piece of artwork, without knowing what was being given. Our little investment was by an Indian artist who was rapidly growing in popularity in the contemporary art world. Several years later, we discovered that Christie's was holding an auction for his work and when Harry got in touch, persuaded us to give them our piece to sell. It sold for a staggering £12,000. We could have paid off some of our mortgage, put it into a savings account or replaced our dilapidated windows. Instead we blew it all on our trip. To this day I wonder if we did the right thing (it certainly wasn't the sensible thing), but it's a holiday which none of us has ever forgotten and holds some of our happiest memories.

When we got back, Gabriel's mood changed. Although he was now almost seven, it was like living with a demonic toddler. He was stubborn, argumentative and intransigent over the tiniest things: turning off the TV, giving him the wrong socks or pulling the plug out of his bath too soon. He would wail for an hour, or throw things – mostly soft toys – around his room. Sometimes he'd shout – 'I'm so upset. You're so unkind, it's all your fault! I wish I didn't live here.' We exhausted every tactic we shouted back, spoke softly, counted to three, threatened to take things away – 'Right, NO TV FOR A WEEK!' There were never any tears, except ours, usually after we'd shouted and felt terrible. But his screams were so infuriating that I wanted to match them with my own.

Of course, this could have been happening in any other household anywhere in the world with a seven-year-old living in it, but we could never take these bad moods for granted. We always felt a need to question whether there was a deeper, more troubling cause for his apparent unhappiness. Adopted children, we knew, could be sensitive to a whole range of changes that others sailed through. Even those who had been separated from their birth families as babies could be vulnerable to a fear of separation and loss. If this was the case with Gabriel, then he was still too young, perhaps, to either recognise his feelings, or be able to articulate them. Although he did once tell me, in a calm, lucid moment, that he hated himself when he was being difficult.

When Gabriel's mood still hadn't lifted after a few weeks, we decided to call in the experts and get some professional help. Our adoption agency offered post-adoption support, and a friendly play therapist called Jackie came to see us while Gabriel was at school. The first thing she told us was not to call his moods a 'black hole' as it was racist and he might pick up on the negative implications. Moving on, she talked to us about attachment, and the fact that although Gabriel would have considered Mary (his foster carer) his mum since she was his primary carer, he would still have had a strong attachment to his birth mother, which would have been formed in the womb, and have associations with that time – smells, tastes or sounds. When he was moved from his foster carers to us, he would have suffered a severe trauma, which at the time he didn't – and couldn't – express.

'When he has his tantrums, that's where he goes back to. It's very painful for him, so he's expressing his pain,' Jackie explained. She told us not to shut him away, but to keep him near us, to be empathetic and identify that he was feeling bad. We should consolidate our unconditional love too: 'Ask him how you can make things better. Tell him to let you know if there's anything you can do. Let him know that you're trying to keep him close. Don't give in to him, but be kind and calm with him.'

She also suggested we let him listen to his tape of nursery rhymes if he wanted to (sometimes adopted children need to go back to a time when life was more simple), to go through the baby rituals of bath-time, such as rubbing in cream or singing lullabies. I tried later that evening, but fell at the first hurdle when Gabriel insisted on me singing the theme tune to *Ben 10*.

We'd also talked about the Life Story Book. This is the book that every adopted child comes to their adoptive parent with: an account in words and photographs of their life before adoption, including details of their birth parents and family, and, if they're old enough to understand, the reasons behind their adoption. Usually it's made by the social worker close to the child, with the idea that they can bring a personal touch to the story. We were always told that this was an essential tool in helping your child understand their background. Because of bureaucratic incompetence, Gabriel didn't come to us with a Life Story Book, and we spent a year chasing social services to send one. When it eventually arrived, we wondered why we'd been so keen to have it: obviously made by someone who had never met Gabriel, although it wasn't a bad effort, we felt we could do a much better job.

He already had a small photograph album that I'd made for him, which included photographs of his birth parents. We sat on his bed and he looked through all the pictures (he immediately identified his birth mother) and when he got to the end, he said, 'Thank you, Mummy.' He then asked if he could look at it again, so I knew he'd appreciate something more substantial.

Jackie had advised us to make a book that would appeal to a seven-year-old and leave blank pages for him to continue the story if he wanted to – but where to start? I spent days sifting through old photographs and mementos for Gabriel's Life Story Book, indulging in nostalgia. There were his baby footprints taken at birth and a lock of thick hair; his first tooth ('The tooth fairy very kindly gave it back to me,' I lied to him) and a photograph of the hospital where he'd been born; a photocopy of a diary entry written by his foster carers on his last day at their house, and snapshots of his first day at ours. His baby photos made me feel sad that I hadn't been there with him. A set of photographs taken when he was 18 months old to send out to potential adopters made me feel even worse. He looked so sweet and co-operative, smiling for the camera without knowing what was going on. He was so vulnerable, and reliant on the adults around him to do the right thing. I spent even longer deliberating over the words, and what we should write. 'Once upon a time a beautiful baby boy was born…' I began. 'That boy was you.'

He loved it. I know it's the sanitised version of his life – it only shows the happy bits, leaving out the sad – but that's another chapter for another time.

* * *

When Gabriel turned seven I grieved his toddler years. It felt like a milestone: he had moved from Infants to Juniors and was beginning to rely more on his friends for his world view. Taller, more independent, he looked older too. He could get in and out of the bath without help and pour his own milk into his cereal bowl. His vocabulary could still be endearingly confused – 'hicknore' (ignore) and 'alerdrick' (allergic) were our favourites – but also sophisticated. His sentences would start with, 'I suggest' and 'At least'. He had secrets he didn't want to share with us. I felt proud of his confidence: he was out there, doing his own thing and doing it well.

ROSALIND POWELL

I felt this keenly when I saw him compete in a grading ceremony or 'Batizado' in Capoeira, the Brazilian martial art that combines dance and music. He'd been going to classes for about a year, and the Batizado was the ceremony in which students were recognised as capoeiristas and earned their first belt. It was a hot and steamy day inside a hot and steamy sports centre. Gabriel sat in large circle or 'roda' with at least 100 other students ranging in age and size, from kids to adults. Each took his turn in the middle of the circle, sparring with the experienced 'capoeirista', or master. By the time it was Gabriel's turn, my nerves were frayed: he looked so small, kicking out his arms and legs at a tall Brazilian, running circles around him. I started to cry, and then I couldn't stop. I felt so proud – but why the hysterics? Maybe it was at times like these that I should have basked in a reflected glory: after all, this was the sum of our efforts. But could we take any credit for it? It was down to us that he was doing it in the first place, but the confidence to get up and take part was all his own. I was just lucky to observe him doing it this time.

At other times I'd have this sense of foreboding that we only had four years, tops, until he could, potentially, turn into a horrible pre-teen and tell us he hated us. I'd have flashes of this at times when we weren't getting on. When we clashed, I could see a pattern of behaviour developing: he'd say something argumentative, I'd flare up, he'd grow sullen and look at me with dark eyes, I'd shout and feel guilty, he'd sometimes cry. They were intense, short-lived bursts, but I felt they drove a wedge between us. I'd feel distant from him, and would project those feelings onto

193

him. Did he feel he didn't belong? That he'd rather be somewhere else?

We were always waiting for an onslaught of questions about his background and still they never came. Whenever the subject did come up, it was always sporadic, spontaneous, or light-hearted, and I was never prepared.

Messing about one morning, talking nonsense, Gabriel said, 'I want to go home.'

'But you are home,' I said.

'I wasn't born here.'

'Neither was I. So what do you mean by home?'

'With *****,' he said, mentioning his birth mother's name. Of course, when I asked him, he didn't want to talk about it.

'Do you have anything you want to ask me?'

'No.'

'Any feelings you want to talk about?'

'No.'

'Do you think about your birth mother?'

'No, I think about you.' He was feeling guilty, I guessed; playing around with ideas, but he didn't quite know where to take them. But it made me realise we had to take the initiative: we had to make him talk.

I decided to help us both and borrowed a simple picture book about adoption from the library. From the outset Gabriel wasn't interested – in fact, he left it behind when we took his pile of books to the counter. I read it to him when we got home.

'You might feel confused, sad or angry about your adoption,' it read.

'Why would you feel that?' asked Gabriel.

'Well, it's quite sad that your birth mother couldn't look after you,' I explained.

'Not really, as I wouldn't have had you,' he said.

'What a great answer,' I thought. But I also knew I couldn't take it on face value. What if he was in denial? And if so, did it matter? A friend of mine had recently told me that a nurse she knew worked with patients with cancer, and that the recovery rates were apparently better if someone was in denial about their illness. Maybe it was the same with emotional trauma.

Within days my smugness was shattered. We were sitting on the sofa watching *Robin Hood*, in which Robin was having an argument with his half-brother. I explained to Gabriel that they were half-brothers because they had the same mother, but different fathers, and that some families were like that. 'It's like me having two mummies and a daddy,' said Gabriel. 'Well, you have a birth mother and a birth father, then you have a mummy and a daddy,' I said, unprepared and a little defensive. 'So I have two mummies and two daddies?' he asked. At which point I should have just said, 'Yes' and left it at that. Instead I tried, very clumsily, to explain that a birth mother and father weren't the same as a mummy and daddy who are, 'the ones who do the looking after. Are you listening, Gabriel?' 'No,' he said. 'I'm watching this.' Because I'd felt threatened I'd been selfish, and had subsequently confused a seven-year-old with semantics. Luckily, I think he'd lost interest.

A few months later, we went to see *Ice Age 3*. Not a film, you'd think, for which you'd need to feel mentally prepared but it triggered an emotional maelstrom in Gabriel. In the story, Sid, a sloth, stumbles across three dinosaur eggs, which he decides to keep until they hatch. 'Don't worry, I know what it feels like to feel abandoned,' he tells them. I started to feel uncomfortable. How's this going to pan out? When they hatch, he calls himself their mother and they bond. When the baby dinosaurs' mother turns up to reclaim them, there's an emotional scene in which Sid realises he's not equipped to parent the baby dinosaurs and that they belong with their mother. They all bid a sad farewell and go their separate ways.

We came out of the cinema and when I asked Gabriel if he'd enjoyed it, he burst into tears; he couldn't stop. He said he felt sad about the film, and that Sid had to say goodbye, but he didn't want to talk about it any more than that as it made him feel too sad. The following day, it came up again. I told him it was always sad when you had to say goodbye to people, such as when he had to leave all his old school friends behind. I also threw Mary and Bill into the mix, at which point he looked even sadder and said he missed them, and would like to see them. I told him it was fine, I'd arrange it, and he cheered up.

It felt like a hugely significant conversation, but left me feeling uncertain and confused. What was it all about? From which well was he drawing all this sadness? Did he *really* miss Mary and Bill? How could he remember them? He hadn't seen them for five years, since he was two. Did I plant the seeds in his head? Or had the film triggered something? Would it be the right thing to meet up? Was I dictating how he felt by making these suggestions? I wished I knew the right thing to do. I discussed it with Harry, and we decided to see if he brought it up in conversation again.

He did, so I got in touch with Bill and Mary a few months later and arranged to meet up with them in a village near to where they lived. Both Harry and I felt nervous; it felt such a long time since we'd seen them last and we didn't know what to expect – from them, from Gabriel or ourselves. But it was a lot more comfortable and enjoyable than I expected. Gabriel seemed no different; he was pleased to see them, but not overwhelmed, a little hyper and silly, perhaps, but then he had just drunk a can of cola and eaten a packet of crisps. The only time my heart skipped was when Mary told him how he always used to go to sleep listening to music. 'I sometimes used to sing you to sleep,' she said. 'I can't sing for toffee but somehow it worked.' I felt a pang of jealousy, wanting her words to disappear. She also told him he had the silkiest, softest hair when he was born and that a day didn't go by when they didn't think of him. They treasured the photos we sent every year. I was touched that even though they'd fostered as many as 80 children over the years, they still loved him so much.

Despite my jealousy, which I recognised as under-standable but childish, the meeting had been positive and affirming: Gabriel might have lost his birth family, but here were the people who had tried to make up for that loss through their love.

Mary and Bill told us we'd obviously done a brilliant job, as he was such a great child. But if it hadn't been for them, he wouldn't be the child he is now. I knew they could also play an important role in his future, helping him fill in the details about his past. Not so long ago I watched an episode of *Mad Men*, in which Don Draper's daughter

Sally said to him, 'Tell me about the day I was born.' That is a question I'll never be able to answer for Gabriel.

* * *

A couple of months later, I'm helping out at the school summer fair, hulling strawberries with two girls from Gabriel's class. I'm grilling them about the other kids – who's the naughtiest? Who's the most popular? Do the girls ever play with the boys? Then one of them says, 'Emma keeps asking Gabriel if he's adopted.' My heart begins to pound. 'Does she? And what does Gabriel say?' I ask her. 'He says yes. And Rashida asked him if he feels sad that his mum and dad have died.' 'What did Gabriel say?' I ask. 'He just starts singing.' This is one of Gabriel's typical distraction tactics. 'Are you his real mum, or is he adopted?' they want to know. 'Yes, he's adopted and yes, I'm his real mum,' I tell them.

But they've already lost interest. After they've wandered off, I realise my hands are shaking a bit. I wish I didn't always feel so shocked and unprepared whenever the subject unexpectedly comes up. But then being grilled by seven-year-old girls isn't easy. And it served me right for being nosey in the first place. I want to cry for my boy, who has to field all these questions, which he probably doesn't understand, let alone wants to discuss. Are these children kind to him? Probably not. It also breaks my heart that he hasn't told me any of this. Have I prepared him enough? How can I protect him? We hadn't kept it a secret that he was adopted at school, but we hadn't gone around discussing it openly, either. Are we a source of gossip and intrigue?

Later that day I ask Gabriel about it. He tells me yes, some of the girls have been asking him questions. 'Does it bother you?' I ask him. 'Not really,' he shrugs, 'except when they keep asking me the same thing. I tell them yes, I'm adopted, but they just keep on asking.' I try to explain to him that as he gets older, more people will become interested in his adoption: he's special because of it, and they're just curious. He tells me he doesn't feel sad about it. 'I'm happy that I've got a mummy and daddy to look after me,' he says.

So I pluck up the courage to ring one of the girls' mums. I try not to sound critical or accusatory as I ask her to ask her daughter not to question Gabriel again. He doesn't mind people knowing, I tell her, he just doesn't want to be grilled about it. She phones me the next day to say that she's elicited a promise from her daughter, and had a word with some of the other mothers too. I feel relieved. This time, I've been able to step in and help, but I won't always be able to do so. Nor can I help the way it might make him feel.

* * *

There are times when I feel so reassured that Gabriel feels loved, safe, secure and belonging to us that I wonder how I could ever doubt it. I'll get a random note saying, 'You are beutefull (I might have spelt it rong) xxx', or he'll come out with something uncharacteristically profound. Just after his eighth birthday he went on a week-long residential school trip. His excitement was tinged with apprehension about homesickness.

'I can't do anything without you two,' he said.

'What do you mean, anything?' we asked him.

'I can't live without my family,' he explained.

There are times when I know I project my own insecurities onto him. I can be oversensitive about his friendships at school – is he popular? Does he feel liked? Is he being left out? Does he seem different/feel different to everyone else? Does he draw comparisons between his family and that of his friends' and find us lacking?

Then there are the times when I have no idea what's going on in his head. I realised this one morning in 2010. We'd recently acquired a dog, a huge hound that became a trusty sidekick for Gabriel. At first Gabriel had felt ambiguous. A day after the dog arrived, Gabriel, his nose clearly put out of joint, packed a bag with several games, Tiger, his blanket and a Tunnock biscuit and left a note. 'I'm sorry I'm leaving home. Waaah,' it read, with no other explanation. Within an hour he'd changed his mind.

One morning we were in the usual rush to get out of the house and off to school, my constant nagging ringing in his ears. 'Have you brushed your teeth? NO? Then finish your toast, put your shoes on and go to the bathroom. And for the last time, would you put that down, please?' Out of nowhere Gabriel said he felt sorry for our dog as he'd been taken away from his mum, and he wondered if he ever dreamt about her. I explained that pets generally were taken away from their mums, and that we were his parents now. 'No, we're not,' insisted Gabriel. Just as I was wondering if this was the right opportunity to start a discussion, he pre-empted me with, 'I was taken away from my proper mum.' I took a deep breath. 'Well, not your *proper* mum: your birth mum,' I replied. 'But you're not my proper mum,' he said, completely without malice. I reined in my competitiveness, my impulse to say, 'But she's got nothing to do with you now – *I'm* your mother.' Instead I reeled out my stock response: 'Your birth mum grew you and gave birth to you, but I look after you and nurture you, love you and feed you, clothe you and wash you', etc. We were walking to school by now and he'd lost interest.

The conversation had felt like a minefield. It was such a delicate balance, trying to keep my own feelings in check while being honest; using the right words that wouldn't hurt either of us but wouldn't confuse him either; to not get bogged down in semantics, or being politically correct, just accurate. I had to understand that his, 'You're not my proper mum' wasn't a rejection of me, but it still made me feel as if I wasn't legitimate, that I had no right to call myself his mother. Gabriel is so completely my son, but then I don't have another option – he does. He has another mother out there and, maybe, in his mind, she could be so much better than me.

I know I can be oversensitive about being his 'rightful' mother, looking for and finding clues, hints; signs of how I might not be. Gabriel has been learning to play the piano since he was five years old and one morning I heard him playing it downstairs, singing, 'Where Is Love?' from the musical *Oliver!* and trying to pick out the tune. It's a sad, plaintive song about an orphan boy mourning the loss of his mother. How could I not draw comparisons? Or think that Gabriel, subconsciously, was experiencing those very feelings?

At other times it need only be the smallest, throwaway

thing to remind me that our bond goes way beyond the biological. Once, when he was seven, we were sitting doing a jigsaw together. I started humming the theme tune to *Wallace and Gromit*, and he hummed along, tapping his foot. Out of the corner of my eye I saw him get up and start to dance. Still dancing, he turned around and waggled his bottom at me, waiting for me to pat it in time to the tune we were humming. We were both laughing. Is this normal? Is this what other families do? Would social services approve? I wondered.

* * *

Up until very recently, we wouldn't have been able to adopt Gabriel. In fact, it's a small miracle we were able to do so when we did. 'Transracial Adoption' – that is, placing a black, Asian or mixed-heritage child with a white family (or any child with a different ethnicity to the adopter) – wasn't a practice encouraged by social services. The general consensus was that a black, Asian or mixed-race child should only be placed with a family that could reflect its cultural heritage and help steer it through the minefield of racism.

I'm not quite sure why – or how – Harry and I were able to jump through this loophole. When we adopted Gabriel in 2004 , policy was still not in our favour. We are white English – with bits of Irish thrown in – and Gabriel is dual heritage: one of his birth grandparents is African-Caribbean. During the homestudy we had to demonstrate an understanding of cultural and ethnic differences and diversity, and show our willingness to promote a child's cultural heritage if it was different to our own. That wasn't too much of a challenge – we live in a particularly culturally diverse area and have friends of all colours, creeds and races. We don't live in an all-white zone.

But it's not so easy as that. Gabriel has the sort of colouring and features that aren't easy to place – he could be from Egypt or Spain as easily as Barbados or Nigeria. Even so, he will be defined as non-white and, as such, vulnerable to racism. He also looks nothing like us, which isn't a problem for Harry or me but could reinforce in Gabriel a sense of difference, or 'otherness' to us. We have always talked about our skin difference – his lovely brownness compared to our mottled pink. It's more difficult to talk in detail about his cultural heritage because there's not much we know about it. But I understand that one day he may choose to define himself as black.

His perception of himself, and his skin colour, has changed over the years. More recently, as he's grown older, he's said that he wished he could be 'more black'. When I asked why, he said, 'I just do.' Around the same time, he told Harry and me that we were 'racist' for not believing in God. He felt differently when he was younger. Once, when he wasn't well, he observed, 'You can tell when brown people are ill because their face goes white.' I told him his skin was beautiful. 'But I wish I had the same colour skin as you and Daddy, because then I'd look like you,' he told me. It was the first – and only – time he'd ever mentioned this desire to be the same as us. 'Oh, you don't want to have skin like ours,' I said. 'Yours is much nicer.' Was this the wrong thing to say? Did I ignore the underlying insecurities? Probably, but it had caught me unawares.

I tried to bring the concept of his skin colour, and its

origin, to life a bit more. First, we looked at the Caribbean islands on a map. Next, I tried to explain the family line through which he inherited his colour – I drew a picture of his birth grandparents, and his birth mum and dad, and wrote their colour next to them. 'But where are you and Daddy?' he asked, so I drew us. We managed to have a bit of a laugh over my bad drawings, and he seemed to enjoy it, but I could tell he was uncomfortable. He squirmed next to me, at the same time pushing up against me and then pushing me away, almost toppling me over. Then he said, 'But I'm still your darling boy, aren't I?' I told him he'd always be our darling boy, and that the day he came into our lives was our happiest. He asked me to scratch his back and we moved on to something else.

The night before that conversation we'd gone to the cinema to see *Kung Fu Panda 2*. Like the *Ice Age* series, the simplicity of an animated film with its anthropomorphic talking animals, underlying morality and tales from the school of hard knocks could be surprisingly profound. Po the Panda has been adopted by Mr Ping the goose after his parents were (supposedly) killed in battle. Towards the end of the film, Po attains inner peace when he is forced to confront his tragic past. Mr Ping tells Po that his life may have had a sad beginning, but that it didn't define him: what was important was the rest of his life, who he was and how he was going to be.

Chapter Ten

L ike all parents, I worry about my child's future. Will
he make good friends? Will I like them, or the
choices he makes? Will he work hard, take drugs, eat
properly, get into fights, stay out late, fulfil his potential,
discover his talents, give and receive love?

I also have a whole set of other concerns and worries
that can keep me awake at night. Maybe it's because I'm
a natural born worrier, but these anxieties are specific,
I think, to parenting an adopted child. How far will
Gabriel's identity or sense of self be tied in with his adoption?
Will he be troubled by doubts, questions and insecurities?
Will he resent the fact that he's grown up in a white family,
or reject me when he becomes a teenager? Will he want to
trace his birth family? How can I best support him if he
does? And how will I cope when – or if – I feel jealous, or
threatened?

I have other worries (the list is endless) linked to him
being an only child as well. Is he lonely? Does he wish

we'd adopted another child? (The answer to that is 'yes' – he would have loved us to). Is it a burden to have our hopes, dreams and aspirations focused so heavily on him? I reassure myself that he's grown up with four cousins who are like sisters to him and that he's benefitted from our attention, rather than suffered because of it.

For me, being part of a family is about belonging. As parents, we try to create a clan, a tribe, in which we protect and care for each other, and from which we can go out and explore the world and come back home to safety. With adoption, I wonder if this sense of belonging is more complex. Ownership is too strong a word, but I felt I needed to prove myself as a mother before Gabriel could 'belong' to me as my son. Having been taken from not just one but two families – his birth family and his foster family – I wonder how long it took him to feel he belonged to us. And how far does having a different colour skin to us affect this, if at all?

Recently I came across two different accounts of belonging from two adopted writers. One was written by Jeanette Winterson in her memoir, *Why Be Happy When You Could be Normal?* – her account of growing up with her 'monster' of an adopted mother. 'Adoption is outside,' she writes. 'You act out what it feels like to be the one who doesn't belong. And you act it out by trying to do to others what has been done to you. It is impossible to believe that anyone loves you for yourself.' In another passage she describes the 'missing part' shared by all those who have been adopted: 'Adopted children are self-invented because they have to be; there is an absence, a void, a question mark at the beginning of our lives. A crucial part of our story is gone, and violently, like a bomb in the womb.' She adds: 'The feeling that something is missing never, ever leaves you – and it can't, and it shouldn't, because something *is* missing.'

Reading this made me feel a bit hopeless.

Around the same time I heard the author Jackie Kay (who has written, among other books, an excellent memoir about her own adoption, *Red Dust Road*) on BBC Radio 4's *Woman's Hour* talking about her experience of transracial adoption – she is black and her parents are white. Describing her parents as 'kindred spirits', she said the thought of not having been brought up by them frightened her as, 'They felt exactly the right parents for me.' She also said: 'We assume you can only "belong" to people through DNA, but I feel I very much belong to my adopted parents through myths, through stories, through having common interests, through a love of jazz, through memory and experience.'

Listening to this was so reassuring, I almost kissed the radio.

* * *

So what can I do with all my fears and worries, my attempts to second-guess the future and plan for the unknown? The best way, I decided, was to explore them further by talking to other people who had already been through the process. Maybe I could learn from their battles, if they'd had any. So I spoke to adopters and adoptees, young and old, white, black and mixed-heritage, all with different stories and experiences. Talking to them was endlessly fascinating and reassuring. They also helped me understand that parenting, adoptive or otherwise, is down to love, common sense, instinct, trial and error.

'I sound like a crabby old cow but the fact is, I think people fuss about things so much these days,' adoptive mother Margaret, 70, told me. 'What people seem to forget is that people have been adopted for many, many years.'

'If you adopt a child, you expect some stressful stages you have to get through, and you're going to get anxious,' says another adoptive mum, Ginny, 71, 'but you come out the other side, and cope with whatever has happened.'

* * *

My research for this chapter coincided with a raft of reforms to overhaul the adoption system (which I go into in the next chapter). Making adoption a priority, the Coalition Government under David Cameron in 2010 had vowed to get more children adopted from care and to speed up the process that, it claimed, was riddled with delay. A key element would be that speed rather than ethnicity would be prioritised and preventing families from adopting children of a different ethnic group would be 'unacceptable'. In other words, social workers could no longer keep children in care because they couldn't find the perfect ethnic match for them. The figures bore out the facts: black children were taking, on average, over 50 per cent longer to be placed for adoption than those from other ethnic groups. White British children were three times more likely to leave care through adoption than those from ethnic minorities. According to Government statistics (up to March 2011), three per cent of the child population of England were from black or black British and mixed groups. However, 16 per cent of looked-after children were from the same ethnic background. According to statistics from the DoE (up to March 2014), the ethnic breakdown for looked-after children has varied little since 2010.

The practice within social services to find the perfect ethnic match for a child being adopted was a reaction, in part, to the experience of some black children who had been adopted in less enlightened and integrated times by white parents and lived, in isolation, in exclusively white communities.

Mass immigration from Commonwealth countries in the 1950s meant that the cultural and racial mix in many cities became much wider. In the 1960s, the number of black and mixed-heritage children coming into voluntary and local authority care slowly began to increase. But racial prejudice and discrimination prevailed, and the children were automatically excluded from the adoption pool with the belief that the overwhelming majority of white adopters wouldn't want them.

Things began to change in the mid-1960s when the Adoption Project, set up in 1965, sought to establish whether more black children could be successfully adopted by white parents. They advertised for married couples to adopt mixed-heritage infants under 12 months and, as a result, 53 black and mixed-raced babies were placed with 51 mostly middle-class white adopters.

Many middle-class adopters were also sympathetic to the American Civil Rights movement and could see nothing wrong, either socially or politically, with adopting a black or mixed-heritage child. Social policy at the time favoured assimilation rather than recognition of difference and these early adoptive parents were unaware of some of the challenges that they or their children might face: racism in Britain was a lot more explicit in the 1960s and 1970s than now. As a consequence, some black and mixed-heritage children who were adopted in that period have expressed some reservations about their experience.

However, the growing influence of research studies, along with black social workers and lobbyists working in the sector, led to an understanding that cutting a child off from its cultural roots could lead to problems with identity and attachment later in life, so in the 1980s increasing efforts were put into finding black and mixed-heritage adopters who could reflect their adopted child's cultural heritage and background.

Finding the perfect ethnic match for children and adoptive parents became a dominant factor, to the extent that many potential white adopters were discouraged from the start. Harry and I were turned down by one local authority because they weren't looking for white adopters for the mainly black children they were trying to place, who they knew wouldn't be placed with us.

Local authorities are now no longer able to turn down a potential match on the grounds of ethnicity – unless it is deemed in the best interests of the child. Progress is slowly being made.

* * *

When Harry and I were asked during the matching process how we'd try to promote Gabriel's cultural heritage, I'm not sure we really knew what that meant.

I'm still not entirely sure. All we felt we could do, to begin with, was make him aware that he had a different skin colour to us. But at times as he's grown older I've noticed that he's identified himself as 'different' to us – and to others too. Once when we were discussing whether there were any other adopted children at his school, Gabriel claimed there were. When we asked him how he knew, he said it was because some children were a different colour to their parents. For him, skin colour was irrevocably tied with being adopted. We had to explain that this might sometimes be the case, but it wasn't always. But the fact was that he'd spotted these kids and identified with them.

One Christmas we bought him a Wii, on which you can create a variety of characters, or mini mes (or Miis), to play the various games; every character Gabriel chose for himself was black, and the characters he chose for us were white. This intrigued me, so I asked him about it. 'Well, I don't have white skin,' was his simple response. But it bothered me. I know he's not white, but he's not black, either, so why would he choose a black figure?

I put the question to Stephen Marsh, 38, who is of mixed-heritage and was adopted by white parents.

'He hasn't chosen to be that. It's the way he is,' he tells me. 'It's like being gay – it's what you are, it's how you're born; it's not a choice. If you were born with darker skin, in this polarised world that makes you black. With more informed people you can be dual heritage and discuss the merits of that, but society makes those distinctions.'

He is absolutely right, of course, and I felt, on reflection, a bit embarrassed that I hadn't worked it out for myself. Gabriel's skin colour, even if it is of such a tone that makes it difficult to guess his ethnicity, still identifies him as being non-white.

* * *

Maybe I was lucky to speak to the right people who would tell me what I wanted to hear, but I heard mostly positive stories about transracial adoption.

'In social work practice one hears a lot about white people being "limited" in what they can offer children of different ethnicity, but I believe that a good parent can parent any child of any skin colour,' says Josephine, 41, who is African-Caribbean with white adoptive parents and sits on two adoption panels. 'What a child needs first and foremost is to have his/her emotional and physical needs met. In today's society people seem to want to label racial identity as they think it's a positive way of celebrating and owning difference. I personally think such labelling can be unhelpful as all it does is perpetuate concepts of difference and separateness.'

As a baby, Josephine was adopted by Margaret and Richard in 1970 when, she says, transracial adoption fitted the stereotype of 'white middle-class liberals who adopted black children.' Her parents had spent some time in the States in the late 1960s and had been very influenced by the Civil Rights and Black is Beautiful movement. She grew up with two older brothers (her parents' birth children) in the predominantly white area of Wimbledon, south London, and went to a predominantly white school. Incidents of racism, she says, were rare, except once when she was called a 'Paki' – 'I thought, "Well, I'm not even Indian"' – and another time when a woman called out in the street to her mum that her daughter's hair looked a mess. As a child, her family didn't draw attention to, or worry about, the fact that Josephine was a different colour to them.

'I must have been very unimaginative, but I didn't really think it would be a problem,' says Margaret, her mum. 'Occasionally people would make remarks. Someone said to me once, "She's a white child in a black skin" and I said, "That's stupid – I don't even know what that means."'

Nor did her parents actively try to promote her African-Caribbean heritage. 'Which is probably awful,' concedes Margaret. 'But I also take the view that it's quite hard. Josephine's point has always been that children want to be accepted very closely into the family they're in, they don't want difference.'

'I think my mum and dad's main focus was just to give me a very strong sense of an identity – not an ethnic or black identity, but giving me pride in myself and my appearance, like you do with any child,' says Josephine.

'Obviously, ethnicity is a part of who you are, but in my case it's a very small part of my identity. There are people who strongly feel they are black British, and find that a significant part of who they are because of the culture and history. I understand that power – I think as a community and race it's a very specific thing to want to be proud of – but I don't have that feeling at all so I don't identify as anything, apart from just me.'

However, when she hit her mid-twenties, she felt compelled to find out more about her cultural roots, particularly which Caribbean island she was from.

'All my life, growing up I was asked, "Where are you

from?" and I never knew the answer. It was a torment as all I could say was, "I'm from England."'

After accessing her adoption records she discovered that her birth mother was from St Vincent but her curiosity ended there. She was interested in the history of the island, and to some extent the genealogy but, she says, 'I didn't want to know my immediate family. I just wanted an answer to this infernal question, "Where are you from?"'

We're beginning to see an awakening of this in Gabriel. Not so long ago he asked if he was part Jamaican. We said we didn't know. 'Oh, please can I be?' he begged. 'OK,' we said, not knowing whether or not it was the right answer.

But this question of where you're from, your geographical positioning in the world, seems to be a fundamental one for transracially adopted children. Beverley, 46, was brought up in the North of England by white parents, who had fostered her from six weeks old and adopted her, aged seven. Her birth mother was from Barbados and her birth father was Nigerian.

'I felt different – it's the only way I can describe it,' she says. As she grew older, her sense of isolation increased. 'Other kids didn't relate to me very well. It's quite common for black kids to ask each other where their parents are from – in terms of which island in the Caribbean, or what county in Africa. People would ask where my parents came from but I was confused and never knew how to answer that. If I said England, they wouldn't accept it as an answer. Or if I tried to explain I was adopted, I wouldn't know how sympathetic or understanding they'd be. I couldn't really gauge it. I just felt so embarrassed and confused that in the end I would just withdraw into myself and not answer, or put myself in a position not to be asked the question.

'As I came into more and more contact with people who were the same colour as me, I felt more and more isolated. I couldn't relate to what I imagined their home life to be like, and I ended up isolating myself – sort of protecting myself.'

It wasn't something she felt she could discuss with her parents because, she says, 'I knew I couldn't articulate what was going on.'

Did her experience, I wondered, ever make her wish she'd been brought up in a black family?

'If you'd asked me, did I ever wish it, I'd say yes when I was in high school. It would have made life a little easier with some of the things I've experienced – given me an escape route, so to speak. But I was, and am, firmly attached to my adoptive family,' she tells me.

'I never thought, "I'm an ethnic minority in a white family" as you're not seen as that when you're with your family,' says Stephen, 38, who is Jamaican with a mix of Czech and Swiss. Adopted as a baby by white parents, he was brought up in the predominantly white Northeast of England in the 1970s with an older white brother, also adopted. Stephen was adopted in a less open climate than today, and doesn't have the same information to hand as adopted children do now. These days, adopters and children can have access to the whole life history of the birth parent/family as well as Life Story Books and DVDs. In some cases the adopters can meet the birth family too.

Like Josephine, however, his experience has been positive: 'I think waiting for the ideal couple to come along for a mixed-race kid like me is rubbish. I was glad I went to a family who were educated, who gave me a good education as well, rather than [placed with a family that had] anything to do with race,' he says. 'I'd like to shake the hand of the person who put me up for adoption and made the decision to give me to those people because it was a good one.'

I not only want to shake Stephen's hand when he says this but also to give him a big hug. This sentiment is what every adoptive parent wants to hear.

Describing himself as 'mid-range tone', Stephen has encountered racism – even from those closest to him. 'My dad's a church minister and I went to a public boarding school, so I overheard conversations that black people would never hear,' he says. 'I've had friends with me in the car who have been cut up by a black driver and sworn at him in a racist way. Then they say, "Oh, we don't mean you – you're not like that."'

Stephen identifies himself firmly as black, and feels Jamaica is his 'motherland'. 'It's what I'm drawn to naturally. When I was younger and watched cricket, I always wanted the West Indies to win, and I used to play rugby for England, so I know how it feels to play for your country. So I failed the Norman Tebbit's cricket test quite badly,' he says, referring to the phrase coined in 1990 by the Conservative MP, which referred to the 'loyalty' or 'lack of loyalty' of immigrants and their children to the England cricket team. 'You are who you are, and your children have their own ideas, character and perceptions, so as a parent you can't deny your child who they feel they are.'

So if Gabriel wants to identify himself as part Jamaican, who are we to quibble over islands?

* * *

One of my favourite books to read to Gabriel when he was little was *Zagazoo*, a picture book written and illustrated by Quentin Blake about the seven ages of childhood, from baby to teenager. A couple are delivered a baby by stork and watch in shock as it develops from baby elephant to wild warthog to bad-tempered dragon. One day they wake up to discover their child has turned into a 'strange hairy creature' who 'went on getting bigger… and hairier… and stranger'. 'What will become of us?' they wail. But by the next page the strange creature has turned into a delightful young man 'with perfect manners', who makes their breakfast and does their odd jobs.

I'm not looking forward to Gabriel's strange, hairy teenage years, and neither, I think, is he. A friend and his wife, who were having problems with their 17-year-old son, popped round once to see us. Their son used to be a charming, communicative boy like Gabriel, who loved dance classes and playing with Lego; having flunked out of school, he now refuses to look for a job, instead spending his time playing war games on his Xbox and insulting his parents, who are quite keen for him to move out. Gabriel listened to our conversation, intrigued.

'Why is he like that?' he asked.

'Hormones,' we said, and tried to explain the role of testosterone in adolescence.

The next day, clearly troubled, he asked me, 'What if I lose control when I'm a teenager?' I tried to reassure him that his hormones might make him a little moody from time to time, but not to the extent that he'd run wild. I didn't add, 'I hope.'

'I don't want to be a horrible teenager,' he said, still worried.

I look at him, all bright-eyed and bushy-tailed, my little boy who still takes his blanket to bed, lets me read him stories and just about believes in Father Christmas, and sometimes wish I could keep him in aspic.

So what am I so worried about? I understand that adolescent rebellion is a rite of passage. I should know – I was one of those horrible teenagers that Gabriel is so scared of becoming; I argued ferociously with my mum, had unsuitable boyfriends and hated the world generally. If Gabriel behaves in the same way then at least I might be able to understand it. What I feel less prepared for is Gabriel's journey away from us, out into the wider world, and the possible quest to find out where he's from. This may, or may not, involve tracing his birth family.

My fear, which is more rooted in fantasy than any reality, is that contact with his birth family would mean Gabriel rejecting us; that he would make a choice. I don't have another son, but he has another mother. What if, in the midst of any teenage angst, he turns on me to deliver the accusation I dread hearing the most: 'You're not my real mum.' When I exercise logic and common sense, however, I know this isn't likely. It's not even inevitable that he should want to trace his birth family; not everybody does. But if he does decide he wants to do this, then one certainty is that we'll be there for him.

* * *

The 'what ifs?' and possible outcomes for tracing a birth family are endless, and entirely dependent on the individuals involved. There is no one, common adoption experience. For Josephine and Stephen, the desire to find their birth parents has never arisen.

'It's almost like delving into someone else's family,' says Josephine. 'Who are these other people? They've got nothing to do with me. It's unsettling as well to think you have any sort of relationship with a bunch of strangers, just because you've had a biological link to them.'

'I don't want to hear anything about my biological parents,' says Stephen. 'I don't want to know whether my birth father beat up my mother, or [they] were drug addicts, or [had] been to jail or tried to abuse me. That's someone handing over some baggage on to me.

'When I was 18 or 19, I'd occasionally think about the circumstances. "What did my birth mum have to go through to give up her kid?"' he adds. 'But because I'm not one to speculate about a million causes I'd think, "Well, I'll never know and it's probably best that I never do."

'There is that curiosity thing of, "I wonder what my birth mum looks like?"' he admits. 'I'd also be curious to have my own children, to see what they looked like, because I don't know anyone who looks like me. But I wouldn't call my birth mother "Mum" because that's the person who changed my nappy and cleaned up my cut knees, not the person who gave birth to me. I look [on] a birth mother as a surrogate mother, the person who carries the kid but doesn't look after them. It sounds clinical, but the bond you have with a mother is the one you have from time.'

Michelle, 25, who was adopted as a baby and brought up in Essex by Diane and Joe, raises an issue I hadn't even considered with all my speculative ponderings and prophesying.

'My biggest fear is that she'd want to be my mum,' she says of tracing her birth mother. 'I couldn't be someone else's daughter. I could be friends with her, probably, or I could get on with her, but even scarier than her rejecting me would be me breaking this woman's heart.' For Michelle, her curiosity about her birth family is equally matched by fear of meeting them. 'I don't know if I'm brave enough yet,' she admits. 'Twenty-five years is a long time for someone to rebuild their life. What if she's got a new life with a new husband, new children, and they don't know she ever gave someone up? I can't storm into her life and disrupt everything, demanding answers.'

Beverley, although fostered from a baby until she was adopted, had regular contact with her birth mother up until she left the UK when Beverley was seven years old. She didn't hear from her again. When she was 32, Beverley decided to trace her.

'I'd hit a low point and it became clear that some of my emotional problems were around identity,' she explains. 'I wanted to change the way I was feeling and this seemed the best way to start.'

She eventually traced her mother to Barbados, and discovered she had had six children with four different fathers. Having made contact, Beverley flew to Barbados to meet her: 'I was able to get answers to some of my questions – I was able to ask her what time I was born, where my first and middle name came from, that sort of thing. But I didn't ask her why she'd left me as I knew she wouldn't be able to answer the question. Nor did she offer any explanation. My view is that she was emotionally damaged in some way. I sometimes wonder what happened in her upbringing that might have influenced her to make the decisions she made around her children. It's the only thing that made any sense to me, if I'm honest.'

Returning to the UK, Beverley exchanged letters with her birth mother for a while – 'She wrote and asked me for forgiveness, but I found it hard to grasp this concept for a long time. I remember writing back that she would have to forgive herself.' Over time, her feelings softened: 'When I last wrote to her, in 2009, I said I'd forgiven her, that I was lucky to have been raised and loved by my adoptive family, and to have had the life I'd had.' For Beverley, this represented 'closure' and she hasn't written to or heard from her mother since.

Having struggled with her identity growing up, visiting her mother made her feel more 'solid'.

'I got an insight into a life I could have had,' she says, 'and being there made me grateful for the family life I have.'

* * *

So what about the adoptive parents whose children have traced their birth families? Were they riddled with the same fears and insecurities as me? Did they put their own needs to one side, stand back and not interfere? Were they rejected and shut out? Or loved and involved in just the same way they'd always been?

One thing I discovered during my conversations with other parents was the power of the word 'Mum'. Adoptive mothers don't like it being shared or taken away. Having worked so hard to earn it, we cling to it.

'The thought of another mother wasn't a threat because I didn't think it would compete with me,' says Josephine's mother Margaret. Since her daughter has never chosen to trace her birth family, this has never been put to the test. 'Although if it had been, I would have said, "You'd better remember that I'm your mum. You can love anybody as much as you like – and I hope you will – but you will not call anyone else 'Mum'." I think it's a precious word.'

When her son first referred to his birth mother as 'Mum', Ginny felt compelled to correct him. Ginny, 71, and her late husband had three birth children before adopting their son Ben, who is of mixed-heritage and now 38, when he was 16 months old. He had a happy childhood and adolescence, and showed no interest in tracing his birth family.

'He just wouldn't go there; he wasn't particularly curious. Sometimes I'd say, "If you ever want to, that's fine with us," to reassure him, and he'd just grunt at me!'

Ben married, had a daughter and moved to Spain, where he still lives. Around the age of 28 he decided to trace his birth mother: a decision, Ginny believes, encouraged by his wife, who was interested in her husband's background.

'I was worried for him, that it would be emotional. But he was an adult, it was his right to do it, and I'd always told him he should if he wanted to,' says Ginny.

Ben successfully traced his birth mother through an agency and eventually received a letter from her.

'He rang me up and said, "Mum, I've had a letter from my Mum."' And I said, "Just wait a minute – *I'm* your mum."' That precious word again. 'He said, "I'm sorry, I'm sorry."' He showed me the letter – and it was delightful. She said that she'd always thought about him, and didn't want to rush him but would like to get in touch.'

His birth mother hadn't had any other children and as such, their reunion was an intensely emotional one. Over the next few years, Ben met his extended family but, it transpired, his birth mother wasn't as interested in meeting those closest to him, including Ginny.

'She's only really interested in him. She's not got the broader view of his life; she can't fill the gap. He's been brought up by somebody else over many years and for her, it was like she was living with this dream of a child that she lost, so it's quite hard for her. I've said that I'd be interested in meeting her, and all he says is "Hmmm",' she laughs. 'Although if I did meet her, I'd probably be quite emotional about it.'

So how has she felt, watching this relationship unfold, this bond form?

'I'm quite tough, and I think you have to be,' she says. 'I hoped it would be OK for him, and his marriage – but emotionally? I felt threatened, I suppose. You can't help it, especially if someone is going to come and claim their long-lost son. They look alike, their noses are the same – that sort of thing.

'I don't think I ever thought I'd lose him,' she adds. 'We're a close family. But I'm not saying it's easy.'

However, several years later and things have settled down to the point where Ginny no longer feels she needs to ask Ben about the relationship.

'I think he sees her about twice a year, so it's receded somewhat. The initial meeting was so emotional, but then reality sets in and you've suddenly got another person to deal with who's important to you – they gave birth to you, but they don't necessarily fit into the life you've made for yourself.'

As for Ginny, she's no longer feeling quite so 'wobbly'.

'It seems to be fine and we've come out the other end,' she says. 'Things have settled down and I feel very lucky.'

I know my 'survey' was a relatively small one, but I found both the adopters and adoptees I spoke to about tracing birth families immensely reassuring. I also appreciated their honesty – especially the mums. It can't be easy to stand back and watch your child meet up and possibly form a bond with the woman who gave birth to him. The fact that I didn't carry Gabriel and greet him the moment he entered the world is one of my big sorrows. But if he ever wants to meet the woman who did, then I will support him, as any good mother would.

* * *

How far will being adopted shape Gabriel's identity, his sense of self? How far will it define him? And will it ever bother him?

When he's older, I hope I can ask him – if he wants to talk about it, that is. Up until now he hasn't really been able to avoid discussion. We've been encouraged to talk to him about his adoption, and talk we have. But does such openness make things easier, or does it reinforce a sense of difference? Was life simpler when adoption was kept secret, when people weren't told (or not until they were much older) and families closed rank?

Beverley, who was adopted by her foster parents at the

age of seven, also feels that she is defined by her adoption.

'It's made me the person I am,' she says. 'I would not have had the life I've had, or grown up with the people I have, or loved the way I have, if I hadn't been adopted. If you look at all the different lives I could have had… so it's very much tied in with my identity, and who I am.'

For Michelle, being adopted is part of her identity, 'some of the time. I suppose it is so much a part of who I am.' But it has also made her feel special. 'I know who my family is. When [other people] have children, they fall pregnant, and have a baby. My parents had to fight to get me. So as a child I felt quite special because my mum and dad chose me.'

Who knows how far Gabriel will feel defined by his adoption. I hope it's not a source of sadness as he grows older; I hope that if it does make him feel different, it will do so in a positive way, like Michelle.

'I'm a confident, well-rounded young man and have been given a good start in life by really stable parents,' says Stephen. 'So I won the lottery when I was adopted.'

I hope Gabriel will feel some of that.

* * *

Some of my conversations continued long after we'd met. A few weeks after I'd spoken to Josephine, she sent me an email.

'I know you were quite surprised to hear me speak so positively about my experiences but generally it's the people who have had negative experiences who are likely to be the most vocal,' she wrote. 'People like me who have had positive experiences are more likely to keep quiet because it's never occurred to them that there's anything to talk about.'

But it's so important to hear those voices, too. I not only felt reassured by the conversations I had with adopted people, but hopeful. Talking to them was the antidote I needed to go forward with confidence.

'Proceed with a light touch,' Josephine advised in one of our email correspondences. 'Allow Gabriel to feel that being part of your family is where he fundamentally belongs, while also leaving room for openness and discussion about things when he's ready.

'I was born and raised with a strong sense of self,' she adds. 'Give Gabriel his sense of self and he'll be able to handle anything.'

As adopted parents we can get so caught up in doing the 'right thing', or anticipating the next stage, or worrying about the past looming and taking us by surprise. We forget sometimes just to trust our own judgement, follow our instincts, accept our mistakes and have faith in the fact that our love for our children will serve them well.

Chapter Eleven

Much has changed in the adoption world since Gabriel came to us. When we first started out, social media was in its infancy, so communication with fellow adopters could only happen through support groups, if you were lucky to have any in your area, or the time (and energy) to attend them. Since then, the rise of Facebook and Twitter have helped break down barriers, giving adopters a bigger voice and creating a community. Problems can be shared, advice sought, campaigns launched, support groups formed – and you don't have to leave the house. People can express themselves and reach an audience through their blogs. It's a world I didn't have access to, which may – or may not – have helped us in those early days, reminding us there were others out there.

Technology has also played a part in giving potential adopters freer access to children's information on the internet, which was once controlled by the social workers only. Online services such as The Adoption Register – a national database which helps find approved families for children around England – and the Adoption Link have given access to adopters to look for children beyond their local authority.

There are also Adoption Activity Days, at which prospective adopters are able to meet and interact with children waiting to be adopted in a fun, safe environment. Traditionally, adopters read reports and profiles of children, and sometimes see a photograph or DVD, and would only meet the child they were adopting after they'd been matched. This, however, reverses the process, enabling adopters to have a more emotional response, and maybe discover something about a child they might have missed had they just read about them. This chemistry could also lead to adopters looking at children they might not otherwise have considered.

When we adopted, this idea would have been inconceivable. I'm not convinced I'd have enjoyed it either – the atmosphere must be pretty intense. It must also introduce an element of competition – what happens when more than one family is interested in the same child? Nevertheless, these events are successful – according to BAAF (before it merged with Coram in 2015), a quarter of children who attend an Adoption Activity Day are matched with an adopter. It has also become the number one method of finding a family for harder-to-place children. Despite these advances, in the last ten years alone the pendulum has swung in and out of favour for adoption, as seems to be the pattern, and depending on who you talk to, it's either in bad shape or rude health.

A snapshot taken from figures published by the Department of Education (in England and up to March 2014) shows a relatively healthy picture. Of the 68,000-plus looked-after children, most of whom are in care due to abuse or neglect, 5,050 left care through adoption, at an average age of three years and five months: only four per cent of the children were under a year old. Many of the children waited around 18 months on average for a new family.

However, a growing trend to look at alternative but permanent solutions for children in care, coupled with recent court cases questioning the evidence presented for adoption cases, has had a significant impact on more recent adoption figures and sparked one of the most pressing current debates: are there alternatives to adoption that can offer a child the same level of security and stability without severing the tie with their birth family?

For this chapter I spoke to many adoption experts and practitioners to present a general, balanced overview of the current climate. I knew it was a highly complex and emotive issue but I wasn't expecting it to be quite so, well, political. As such I've tried to be objective and to understand that adoption isn't a one-size-fits-all solution for every child in need of a secure and loving home. But I'm also aware that my own positive experience of adopting our son has informed my opinion, and not everyone will share it.

'There's a very good argument in favour of this remarkable intervention which so transforms people's lives,' says Sir Martin Narey, government adviser on adoption, 'but lots of people don't like it.'

* * *

In the last few years, the Coalition Government, and now the Conservative Government under David Cameron, have made a firm commitment to adoption. In his party conference speech of 2011, the Prime Minister vowed to tear up Britain's adoption rules and end the 'scandal' of thousands of children lost in the care system. A raft of reforms were introduced to overhaul the system, based on the evidence that children in care were waiting too long to be placed for adoption and potential adopters were having to wait too long to be matched with a child, and that there was little coherence in practice across the UK. In other words, some local authorities and voluntary adoption agencies were more efficient than others.

The Prime Minister before Cameron, Labour's Tony Blair, had also put adoption high up on the agenda and figures had improved, but had slumped back down to around 3,000 by 2011. It was also taking over two years for a child to be placed from care into adoption, having been removed from their birth family – a long time in a young child's life when evidence had shown that the younger a child is adopted, the better the outcome.

'They were spending two years plus in the system, with prolonged court proceedings, hopes that they'd maybe go home, or different members of the family would be assessed [to look after them] and then discounted,' says Jeanne Kaniuk, managing director of Coram's Adoption Services. 'It's taken quite a while to grasp the mettle that all these assessments need to be done as a matter of some urgency.'

'Adoption was out of favour and in gentle but terminal decline,' Sir Martin Narey tells me. 'Indeed, one very senior, hugely respected figure – who was director of children's services at the time – said that in the 1990s society decided we didn't want adoption any more because it was giving working-class children to middle-class parents. And I think you'll still find some practitioners who still believe adoption is a failure, because we should be doing things to make sure that the birth mother can be successful.'

A former chief executive of Barnardo's, in 2011 Sir Martin was appointed as an adviser on adoption to the Department of Education and the Prime Minister, shortly after publishing a report on the problems of the adoption system for *The Times*. His research and subsequent recommendations informed the adoption reform programme, first driven by Michael Gove, who was adopted, and subsequently Nicky Morgan.

A quicker approvals process for adopters was introduced with an aim for it to take no longer than six months. A new Adoption Support Fund was introduced in May 2015, with £19 million Government funding, offering access to therapeutic services to children for those families who needed it – at any stage of an adopted child's life. Both measures acknowledged that while adoption is a service for children, the needs of adopters shouldn't be ignored either.

'As a sector we really had to fight for that because the Government was obsessed with throwing money at recruitment of adopters,' says Satwinder Sandhu, who, as well as being our former social worker, was director of adoption and fostering at PACT for five years and is now director of operations at The Homefinding & Fostering Agency. 'There were lots of people out there, saying,

"We've adopted kids from the care system and been left to get on with it, but it's really difficult."'

Money was invested in local authorities to improve services and recruit more adopters. The need for social workers to match on an ethnic basis was also removed: local authorities could no longer turn down a potential match on the grounds of ethnicity – unless it was deemed in the best interests of the child. At the time white children in care were three times more likely to be adopted than black children. As a result of the reform programme, adoption figures rose to record levels, reaching a peak of more than 5,000 children in the year ending March 2014 – an increase of 63 per cent in three years.

So, all well and good. But in September 2013, a ruling made by the president of the High Court Family Division – one of the UK's most senior judges – had a devastating impact and figures subsequently plummeted. Referring to a couple of adoption cases that had come before the courts, he said that judges were becoming increasingly alarmed at the frequency with which children were being put forward for adoption when less 'drastic' measures, such as being cared for by relatives, hadn't been considered. He criticised the 'sloppy practice' of social workers who had not carried out thorough enough investigations into the alternatives which wouldn't break up families. Adoption, he said, was a 'very extreme thing', which should only be seen as a 'last resort'.

His comments sparked confusion throughout local authorities, leaving many convinced they had to try every single extended family member before putting a child up for adoption. So much so that a 'myth buster' guide had to be issued by the Adoption Leadership Board to emphasise that social workers only had to consider all other 'realistic' options before embarking on the adoption process, rather than every possible option. It also stressed that the judgements had in no way altered the legal test for adoption.

But the damage had been done and between September 2013 and June 2014, the number of children being put forward for adoption fell by 47 per cent. Potential adopters who had come forward following a successful recruitment drive were left waiting for children to adopt – at the end of December 2014, 3,130 approved adopters were waiting to be matched. Meanwhile, the number of people registering to adopt children fell by nearly a quarter in the space of three months.

'It was awful,' says Sir Martin Narey. 'It caused a collapse not just in placement orders but in local authority confidence.'

With another couple of cases coming under similar criticism in court rulings at the beginning of 2015, it was clear that the message being sent, certainly from a legal perspective, was that adoption is a draconian measure that should only be considered as a last resort.

'In Britain there is a strong view among quite a large section of the public – and that goes through all layers of society up to the judiciary – that it's simply wrong to remove children from the family they were born into,' says Jeanne Kaniuk. 'You may have to protect them by placing them in a more suitable environment, but that doesn't give you the right to sever that tie.'

'Legally severing a child's relationship with its birth

family is probably one of the most significant things that the state can actually do,' says John Simmonds, director of policy, research and development at CoramBAAF. 'The enormity of that decision is always present, but it's driven by what we know about children's development and their need for a lifelong, secure, loving family life. If it's the right thing to do, it's the right thing to do.'

* * *

One of the most fascinating things I discovered while researching this chapter is that Britain is one of the few countries in the world to allow non-consensual adoption. The States has a similar model – although it's less regulated than the UK and has more private adoptions – but in many parts of Europe it's considered ethically wrong to terminate parental rights. If children are removed from their families, they are placed in care and if they are adopted, this is only done with parental consent. The majority of adoptions in these countries are international adoptions, although these have fallen over recent years.

According to Julie Selwyn, professor of child and family social work at the University of Bristol, Britain probably has, 'The best adoption system in the world, in terms of assessment, and for many families (although I know not for everybody), really good support. But we never shout about it,' she says. 'We're typically British and say, "It's all a bit crap."'

But the European system – or lack of it – has offered another perspective on adoption and helped influence and inform opinion in the UK. Another factor has been the growing number of family rights groups and academics in the social work field who are advocating for children to remain in the family environment, with support given to birth parents to help them cope and, if necessary, rebuild their lives. Projects such as the Family Drug and Alcohol Court run by Coram, for example, helps parents stabilise or stop using drugs and alcohol to keep families together, where possible.

'For some of these people, if those services are there, they can turn their lives around,' says John Simmonds of CoramBAAF. 'But there are some birth families where the risk they pose is horrendous and adoption is the only child-centred option in these cases.'

'Obviously, if parents can get help from their own families then none of us would be advocating removing them, and if you can support parents to change, then great,' says Coram's Jeanne Kaniuk. 'But if you can't, in my view the child-centred thing to do is provide them with as close as you can to the kind of emotional and legal security that other children take for granted.'

'I'm not suggesting that social workers should be cavalier and charge in and take every child, or that birth mothers should be neglected,' says Sir Martin Narey. 'But we leave children in terrible situations for far too long. And it frustrates me sometimes because if we extended out the general aspirations we have for our own children to the children we neglect, we'd remove many more of them.'

Long-term fostering is one way of offering greater stability to a child in care. Another is kinship care, when a grandparent, close relative or even friend looks after the child instead of a birth parent under formal arrangements;

commonly a Special Guardianship Order issued by the court. The benefits of kinship care is that it can offer a child a form of stability without legally separating them from their parents while keeping them within the extended family network. But there are also concerns that these care arrangements are being used when adoption would be better.

'What people are failing to discuss openly, in my view, is that most of the kids we're talking about come from highly dysfunctional families,' our former social worker Satwinder Sandhu tells me. 'So why would you then think that a grandparent, sibling or cousin is going to do any better than the mum or dad? But people are afraid to voice the fact.

'You have to be sure that the circumstances in which a child is being placed, whether it's family, friends or adopters, are superior to where they would have been left. But I have often heard people say, and witnessed, that the courts, or independent social workers, will sometimes make compromises when it comes to kinship care because of this overwhelming feeling that being left with family or friends is better than being placed with strangers.'

'Kinship carers include some pretty fantastic people and we could [help] equip relatives to do a good job, and so we should,' says Sir Martin Narey. 'But when I meet a lot of practitioners, their complaint is that the courts agree to Special Guardianship Orders when the professionals think unequivocally that adoption would be the best option for a child.' He knows of two local authorities, he adds, who have been directed to consider people living abroad as potential kinship carers.

Research carried out by Julie Selwyn of the University

of Bristol in 2014 showed that only three per cent of adoptions disrupted (or broke down), whereas disruption rates for Special Guardianship Orders were double that and, unlike adoption, broke down quickly within two years. But as adoption numbers have fallen, the numbers of Guardianship Orders have increased.

'The kinds of kids who are adopted in England – and this is a bit stereotypical – tend to come from families where the mothers have been brought up in care themselves,' Selwyn tells me. 'These are not mums with loads of support networks and nice, happy families who are going to be willing to step in. There are drug abusers, alcohol issues, people with mental health issues, learning difficulties, who have been in care themselves, so the simplistic idea that all we need to do is support extended families doesn't help us very much.

'I don't understand it because I come from a children's rights perspective – that children have the right not to be abused, that every child should have the right to grow up in a loving, caring family and that, as parents, we have responsibility for our children – we don't own them.'

* * *

So what next for adoption? Which way will the pendulum swing? Sir Martin Narey is cautiously optimistic for a 'complete or partial recovery' from the recent drop in adoption figures.

There have been some positive signs. In July 2015 the British Government pledged £30 million to help speed up finding adoptive parents for children in care in England by helping authorities to locate people outside their local area. The change was welcomed as a 'bold move' by Coram. However, at the time BAAF (before it merged with Coram in 2015) stressed there was an 'urgent need' to address the fact that many children in care had 'a range of complex issues' which made it difficult to find adopters. Many adopters are still looking for a healthy, single child under the age of two. But of the 3,000 children waiting to be placed, many are considered the 'harder to place' – i.e. over four years old, disabled or with serious health conditions, or need to be placed with siblings or from black or minority ethnic communities. Many wait much longer for a family to be found. But the question remains, how do you encourage people to come forward and adopt these children who are waiting and who have such challenging needs?

'It's a difficult balance,' agrees Jeanne Kaniuk of Coram. 'There are people out there who, when they hear about [these] children feel it is something they can do. And a lot of people who apply to adopt say that one of the things that irritates them is the amount that social workers try and put them off. But you have to be honest. There's no point luring people in who are then terribly out of their depth and disappointed.'

'It is important that prospective adopters have opportunities to explore their views about the children they feel they can adopt,' says John Simmonds of CoramBAAF. 'The images that are stirred up by terms like "disability", "two or three children rather than one", "a three-year-old" rather than a one-year-old, can create uncertainty and anxiety. But they are all children at heart.'

The fact that there are still vulnerable children in care

and in desperate need of a long-term, secure family life is an issue, he adds, that, 'has to keep us up at night'.

And for Julie Selwyn of the University of Bristol, adoption offers the best solution: 'All the research from around the world shows that adoption produces good outcomes. If we got rid of adoption then what for these children? What hope are we going to give them? What kind of lives are they going to lead? What sort of options are they going to have? Growing up in a family is your best option in life, and if you haven't got a birth family that can offer support, then an adoptive family is the next best thing.'

* * *

I wanted to end this chapter on an upbeat note, and to highlight the transformative effect of adoption on one particular family. Theirs is a unique story, but also an inspiring one.

In 2015 Julie and Roger Elliot were awarded an MBE for services to adoption. For the past 32 years the couple, who live in large, converted barn in a small village in Lancashire, have had four adult birth children and adopted nine children with disabilities of varying degrees. Robert, 33, and Jonathan, 25, have Down's syndrome; Steven, 23, was left profoundly disabled after being shaken as a baby; Colin, 12, has severe learning difficulties and his twin, George, has cerebral palsy; Dante, five, has very mild cerebral palsy on his right side; Amelia, six, has cerebral palsy, as does three-year-old Lucas. Their son Devon, who had cerebral palsy and a congenital heart defect, died two years ago, aged 19. Three of the children use wheelchairs and, apart from

Dante, who's, 'like every other five-year-old', they are unlikely ever to lead independent lives.

Apart from their eldest son Sam, 32, who works in politics, their other three children – James, 30, Natalie, 28, and Alexander, 26 – work in the caring professions.

I can't even begin to imagine what it must be like to care for these children with such profound needs and without help (except for a cleaner), but Julie, 55, who is charming and funny, is clearly in her element. So what are the qualities that have enabled her to take the job on?

'Patience, a sense of humour, not expecting too much but enjoying what you get,' she explains. 'We enjoy the company – they really are such special kids.

'They don't let anything get them down. Everything they achieve, they've had to work really hard for, and everything is a pleasure to them. They don't judge people. All they know is whether people are kind to them, and everybody is their friend. That's what makes them special.'

Describing herself as a 'fusspot parent', she admits she also likes to feel needed.

Both former nurses, Julie and Roger have a wealth of practical and medical experience between them. They first met when they worked in what used to be called 'mentally handicapped' hospitals, where patients were institutionalised and rarely got beyond the hospital gate.

'We were working on the children's ward and we used to sit and say, "There must be something better than this. These children deserve more."'

They first approached a local authority in 1981 to see if they could adopt a child with a disability, but, 'We were made to feel odd,' says Julie. 'They couldn't understand us and were like, "We don't want people doing it for the wrong reasons". But nobody told me what [the wrong reasons] were – I still don't know.'

It wasn't until 1989, when their local authority did a recruitment drive for adopters for hard-to-place children, when Julie felt they were 'taken seriously' and began to build their extended family.

They could, in theory, have carried on working with disabled children or considered long-term fostering. 'But I think [our children] deserve the permanency of adoption. And I'm not cut out for work,' says Julie, who looked after the children on her own at home until Roger took early retirement, five years ago. 'I'm not very good at being told what to do, and struggle with authority, which is why I couldn't foster, as I like to be able to make the decisions. I'd also find it hard to let the children go when they had to move on.'

Managing a household with eight kids – as well as four Shetland ponies, two dogs, a cat, chickens and geese – requires excellent organisational skills and an ability to keep calm. Mornings are staggered – the children, who all have their own bedrooms, get up at different times – and only Lucas is at home during the day. They have a wheelchair-accessible bus for travel but it's still a challenge if they all want to go out together.

'We're very lucky that our birth children come with us when we go on holiday. We can clear an airport café in about five minutes. We'll walk in and my daughter will say, "There's nowhere to sit, Mum," and I'll go, "There will be in a minute,"' she deadpans. Roger will sometimes go on a cycling holiday with friends and Julie visits a friend with a villa in Spain but the idea of 'me time' is an anathema.

'People say, "What about time for yourself?" and I think, "I don't know what you mean." I always find it quite baffling when people have children and complain. What do they think is going to happen when they have a child?'

Julie appreciates that because of their past nursing experience, she and Roger know what they're doing and what to expect. She also understands that adopting a disabled child is a very different parenting challenge to adopting a healthy one.

'If you can't conceive and adoption is your way of starting a family, you have all these dreams and aspirations for your children and many of those things you can't do with a disabled child,' she concedes. 'I would have been exactly the same.'

However, she gets frustrated by some of the negative messages given to potential adopters. In the past she's been asked for advice about how best to recruit more adopters for disabled children.

'I always say, you can't change people's minds. You can't expect people who want to adopt a so-called "normal" child to suddenly have a big revelation and change of heart, because the two things are very far apart.

'The other theory I have is that social workers get so hung up on the disability and medical aspects they forget to present the child. When we were being matched with our children, the way the social worker spoke about them you'd think they needed to be in intensive care, not a family, because they couldn't see beyond their disabilities.

'I'm sure there are lots of people out there who would be brilliant with a little one with some sort of disability, but they're led to believe that it's something only special people can do.

'None of us are born parents,' she continues, 'we all learn as we go along, but the expectation is that these skills will be there ready and waiting, and it's not realistic. There's this myth that people have to be special but you've got to let them learn as they go along. If they were more open to that, more people would give it a go.'

Chapter Twelve

When I started to write this book, Gabriel was six and a half years old. But my story of him (although not the book) ends just before his tenth birthday. I didn't think it was fair to write about him beyond that age, as he grows older and more conscious of his place in the world.

He's not the child he was when I first started writing. There's an added depth and poignancy to our relationship now that comes from him growing up, growing away and growing in independence. He does things without being asked, or helped: he gets dressed, makes his own breakfast, sometimes even his own packed lunch. Every morning he makes me a cup of tea in bed. I respect his growing maturity and individuality, value his opinion (on some things) and we meet more as equals.

Sex, love and babies made a brief entry into the conversation... and then a quick exit. 'Where are the three lady holes again?', 'If a man can marry a man, can they have sex?', 'What if I love someone and they don't love me?' and 'Does it hurt when a lady has a baby?'

Of course he's still very much a child. Just before his tenth birthday, in a serious voice, he listed his skills: being able to touch his nose with his tongue; being double-jointed; being able to do an eyebrow wave (raise one after another); and doing a front flip on a trampoline without using his arms and still landing on the diamond on his backside.

The changes, both within the adoption field and in Gabriel, have given me cause to reflect on my book. The climate – and system – might be different to when Harry and I were first assessed and approved to be adoptive parents, but the emotional journey, I'm sure, will still be a common experience. As such, I hope my story can help or interest those who are about to embark on it, or have also shared the experience.

My feelings about the book and Gabriel are more complex. From the start I have questioned whether I should be writing about him and, as he gets older, I question this more. When he was smaller he had little or no concept of this project. Now he does, but he still has no choice over it. So, am I exploiting him? Will he resent me when he's older? Will he feel exposed? It's one of the reasons why I chose to change his name – as much as it's hard for me to write about 'Gabriel' when his real name is so much part of him, I felt I needed to give him a degree of anonymity. It's the same with most of the other adopted children and adoptive parents I've written about in the book: I've used different names to protect their privacy.

I recently read a lecture given by the American novelist

and essayist Jonathan Franzen, published in *Farther Away*, a collection of essays, in which he talked about the writer's dilemma in mining their family and friend's lives for material. He talked about using elements of his brother's life for one of his characters in *The Corrections*: 'The benefits of being on good terms with your friends and family are obvious and concrete; the benefits of writing about them are still largely speculative. There comes a point, though, when the benefits begin to equalize. And the question then becomes: am I willing to alienate somebody I love in order to continue becoming the writer I need to be?' He adds: 'What turns out to matter most is that you write as truthfully as possible. If you really love the person whose material you're writing about, the writing has to reflect that love. There's still always a risk that the person won't be able to see the love, and that your relationship may suffer, but you've done what all writers finally reach the point of having to do, which is to be loyal to themselves.'

I found this hugely reassuring. I do hope that when Gabriel is old enough to read this book (should he want to) that he will recognise that it's been written with love, about love.

* * *

After talking to adopted people for this book I stopped worrying quite so much about how much or when I should be talking to Gabriel about adoption. Not that I was constantly badgering him about it, but I felt reassured that it didn't have to be a central or defining part of our life; I wanted to let him be.

However, I wanted to end this book with his voice. I've written about him, I've talked to other people about him, and so I thought it was time to hear from the subject himself – but how to go about it? I decided to approach it professionally and request an interview with him. He agreed. I gave him a rough outline of the sort of questions I'd be asking, and we arranged a day and time.

It was after school one very hot afternoon just before his tenth birthday. We sat in the garden and he sucked on a fluorescent blue ice pop ('How can it be raspberry flavour?'), wearing shorts, desert boots and socks, pulled up high. It was a miracle he wasn't wearing a vest – he likes to dress warmly, even in a heatwave. The formal structure of the interview helped us both: the tape recorder acted as a buffer and he could talk to his mum as a journalist. I didn't know what to expect: he is generally reluctant to be drawn into analytical discussion, especially about adoption. But I was surprised, and touched, at how prepared he was and the thought he'd put into some of his answers.

I take a deep breath (I actually felt quite nervous) and ask him how he feels about me writing a book about us, and adoption.

'I think it's nice because I'm lucky to have such a nice mum and dad, but,' and here he pauses, 'sometimes I think of me being adopted and I feel a bit sad that I never got to meet my birth parents, really.'

Deep breath.

'It makes you feel sad? What sort of things do you think?'

'That I never really met them, I only see them in pictures. I only met them when I was a baby. I've been passed on from two homes to the third one. The first was with my birth mum and dad, and then I was at my second home, and now this one.'

I take another deep breath. 'Well,' I tell him, 'I think that's probably how a lot of adopted people feel about it, happy and sad at the same time.'

'Well, not at the same time: separately,' he corrects me. 'Sometimes I feel happy that I'm adopted, because I've ended up with a nice mum and dad who have loved me and looked after me, and then sometimes I'm just a bit upset, really.'

At this point I want to cry. Never before has he expressed such an awareness of his journey through different homes; how he'd been 'passed' from one to another. I couldn't bear the thought of him feeling unhappy but at the same time I also felt proud of his ability to articulate his feelings and not be afraid to do so. I ask him if there are any particular times when he feels sad.

'Sometimes when I look at photos of them, it makes me feel sad. I think, "What are you like? Why can't I meet you?" I've got quite a few photo albums.'

I try to reassure him that if, when he's grown up, he still wants to meet them, then we can try to find them and that we would help him.

'Yeah, yep,' he says, quietly.

Gabriel has never minded people knowing he's adopted, and I want to check this is still the case.

'No, I don't mind,' he says, shaking his head. 'I don't mind talking about it. It's just when people want to talk to me about it too much, especially when I don't feel like it.'

I tell him that's fair enough, and that he has every right to say if he doesn't want to. But I can tell he's starting to lose interest and has got a bit fidgety, so I quickly squeeze in another couple of questions.

'Could we love him in a better way?'

'No, you can't be a better Mummy and Daddy. That would be merely impossible.'

'Really?'

'Merely, yes,' he says, savouring his current favourite word.

I sometimes wish that we'd had him from when he was first born. Does he ever wish the same?

'Sometimes,' he nods. 'But I don't really mind because I'm with you now.'

A couple of days later I ask what he meant when he said he felt lucky. I'm not fishing for compliments, or seeking reassurance, I just want to know what he means by luck.

'I just think you're the best mum and dad I could ever have,' he says. 'I've seen other friends' mums and dads and if I had to choose, I'd still say you.'

'What's so great about us?' I ask, milking the moment.

'Well, you're kind,' he says. 'And you only shout when you really need to.'

* * *

There were parts of that conversation I found difficult to hear. It's so much easier for me, and Harry, to think that everything's fine; the past can be forgotten, our love will make up for his loss. But if we demand honesty from him, then we have to accept his answers, however hard they might be to hear. It's a conversation we will, hopefully, continue to have.

Much has happened since Gabriel arrived as a toddler.

ROSALIND POWELL

If I project forward, I struggle to imagine him at 18. What will the next few years bring? What will he be doing? Where will he be? How will we be getting on? I worry that our adoption journey so far has been too easy, and that I'm not prepared should events take a different turn, or the solid foundations of our relationship begin to crumble. Adolescence is around the corner and, like all parents, Harry and I are preparing for a possible bumpy ride. I hope there will be just pot holes, not black holes.

I remember hearing or reading somewhere one of those natty but negative adoption sound bites (it could have been the title of a documentary or book), which was, 'Love is not enough'. Maybe the future will bear this out but I doubt it: I believe love goes a long way.

And as for that fundamental question, 'Can I love a child that isn't my own?'

How could I have loved anybody as much as I love my son?

Bibliography/References

BOOKS

Furse, Anna. (1997) *The Infertility Companion*. Thorsons

Keating, Jenny. (2008) *A Child for Keeps: The History of Adoption in England, 1918-45*. Palgrave MacMillan

Elliott, Sue. (2006) *Love Child*. Vermillion

van Gulden, Holly & Bartels-Rabb, Lisa M. (2004) *Real Parents, Real Children*. The Crossroad Publishing Company

Verrier, Nancy. (2009) *The Primal Wound: Understanding the Adopted Child*. BAAF

Figes, Kate. (2008) *Life After Birth*. Virago UK

Golombok, Susan. *Modern Families: Parents and Children in New Family Forms*. Cambridge University Press, 2015

Quinton, David. (2012) *Rethinking Matching in Adoptions from Care: A Conceptual and Research Review*. BAAF

Smith, Carole & Logan, Janette. (2003) *After Adoption: Direct Contact and Relationships*. Routledge

Triseliotis, John & Feast, Julia & Kyle, Fiona. (2005) *The Adoption Triangle Revisited*. BAAF

Owen, Morag. (1999) *Novices, Old Hands and Professionals: Adoption by Single People*. BAAF

de Jong, Anisa & Donnelly, Sharon. (2015) *Recruiting, Assessing and Supporting Lesbian and Gay Adopters*. BAAF

Howe, David. (1996) *Adopters on Adoption*. BAAF

Jarratt, Claudia Jewett. (1994) *Helping Children Cope with Separation and Loss*. The Harvard Common Press

Morris, Ann. (1999) *The Adoption Experience*. Jessica Kingsley Publishers Ltd

Fahlberg, Vera. (2004) *A Child's Journey Through Placement*. BAAF

OTHER SOURCES: Reports, newspaper reports and online resources:

The Narey Report on Adoption: Our Blueprint for Britain's Lost Children. The Times, Tuesday 5th July 2011

Jim Wells resigns as Northern Ireland Health Minister
    http://www.bbc.co.uk/news/election-2015-northern-ireland-32476991

http://www.theguardian.com/uk-news/2015/apr/27/
jim-wells-resigns-northern-ireland-health-minister

Domenico Dolce and Stefano Gabbano comments "The only
family is a traditional one" in report in *The Sunday Times*,
22nd March 2015

Watson, Ken. Meeting the Challenge of Successful Adoptive
Parenting: A New Way of Looking at Adoption

Slomnicka, Barbara Irena (2014) Adoption: A Gallop
Through History
    www.fourteen.co.uk/wp-content/uploads/2014/05/
ADOPTION.doc

The history of the NHS in England in the 1960s http://
www.nhs.uk/NHSEngland/thenhs/nhshistory/Pages/
NHShistory1960s.aspx

Foundling Hospital: http://www.coram.org.uk/our-
heritage-foundling-hospital/foundling-hospital-and-social-
care-historical-context

Forced adoption: The mothers fighting to find their lost
children
    The Guardian (Society), October 2013

Selman, Peter: Towards a Demography of Adoption: making
sense of official statistics on child adoption and the search
for origins
    Paper presented at the Second International Conference
on Adoption, University of East Anglia, Norwich, July 2004

"Gay weddings" become law in the UK
BBC News, December 2005

Understanding Attachment Problems and Disorders,

HelpGuide.Org
http://www.helpguide.org/articles/secure-attachment/attachment-issues-and-reactive-attachment-disorders.htm

Burnell, Alan. Explaining Adoption to children who have been adopted (Discussion paper, Post-Adoption Centre)

Local Authority Circular LAC(98)20

Changes for mixed-race Adoption Policy
BBC News and Education, 22nd February 2011

Children in Care in England: Statistics, May 2012 (House of Commons Library)

Selwyn J. Meakings S. and Wijedasa D. (2015) Beyond the Adoption Order: challenges, interventions and disruption. London BAAF.

Jan Banks & Roe Lovelock: Supporting vulnerable children to manage change (2007)

Jan Banks & Roe Lovelock: Understanding adopted children's behaviour in school that may be a barrier to learning (2005)

Corrigan, Mary. Talking to Children about Adoption. Compiled for Childlink Adoption Society

CoramBAAF Adoption & Fostering Academy statistics
http://www.baaf.org.uk/res/statengland

Getting Adopted is straightforward – as long as you're a healthy white baby
The Telegraph, July 2015

Cameron Promises to Transform Adoption

The Times, October 2011

Adoption has to come back into fashion
  The Independent, July 2011

Adoptions Czar to fight for rights of children
  The Times, October 2011

Impact of Court Judgements on Adoption: What the
judgements do and do not say (Myth Buster guide)
  National Adoption Leadership Board, November 2014

Fall in Children being Approved for Adoption Continues
  Children & Young People Now, June 2015

Top Judge pledges to end culture of secrecy at Family Courts
  The Telegraph, November 2013

Adoption and fostering: 'The Best thing you have Ever
Done'
  The Guardian Society, March 2015

Judge's Ruling blamed for Shock Fall in Adoption Rates
  The Independent, May 2015

Number of Children up for Adoption halves
  BBC News and Education, November 2014

Warning over 'marked' Adoption fall rate
  BBC News and Education, May 2015

FURTHER READING ABOUT ADOPTION:

Donovan, Sally. (2013) *No Matter What*. Jessica Kingsley Publishers

Kay, Jackie. (1991) *The Adoption Papers*. Bloodaxe Books

Kay, Jackie. (2011) *Red Dust Road*. Picador

Home, A.M. (2008) *The Mistress's Daughter: A Memoir*. Granta Books

USEFUL WEBSITES

http://www.adoptionregister.org.uk
http://www.adoptionuk.org
http://www.baaf.org.uk
www.coram.org.uk
http://pactcharity.org
www.first4adoption.org.uk
http://www.familyfutures.co.uk
http://homefindingandfostering.co.uk/
www.education.gov.uk
http://movementforanadoptionapology.org
http://www.youngminds.org.uk/for_parents/services_
children_young_people/camhs

Acknowledgements

A huge thank you to:
My mum Maureen, my sister Sandy and my late dad Syd for their love and sense of humour

Satwinder Sandhu, without whom I wouldn't have my son, and for always reassuring me that I'm doing the right thing

Stacey Thomson, for giving me such a gift of a title and whose reading, re-reading and careful editing of my book improved it no end

All the brilliant adoptive parents and adopted adults for being so generous with their time and for sharing their stories with me, especially Josephine Scorer

All my friends and colleagues who have encouraged and supported me over the years, especially:

Jo Griffin, whose feedback and cheerleading, throughout both the adoption and writing process, helped keep me going; Sally Gatley for her insightful comments and listening skills and Sunita Singh, for being such a good friend for so long

My agent Juliet Pickering at Blake Friedman for her unflagging support and belief in the book from the start, and for Naomi Leon for encouraging me to write it in the first place

Emily Thomas at Blink for saving it from the confines of my desk drawer

But, most of all, to my husband and son, the loves of my life.